How to Praise the Lord

How to Praise the Lord

By

Charles C. Trombley

Contents

Scripture quotations from King James Version and New American Standard.

Introduction

Praising the Lord should be of utmost interest to the heart of every believer. It is indeed of great importance. For praise blesses the heart of God. He delights in the praises of His people. In fact, as the author points out, "He inhabits the praises of His people." That is, He dwells and manifests His power where the people of God are lifting up praise unto Him.

There is much to be said on the subject of praise. A great deal has been said, some of which is good and some of which is in error. We need to be Scriptural in this matter as in all others. We can't afford to get off on a tangent, even in praising the Lord.

I encourage you to study carefully what the Word of God has to say about praise. Read what this author has to say. Read it carefully. Read it all. And then make praise a greater part of your Christian life.

Praise the Lord,

KENNETH E. HAGIN

Chapter One

I Found It!

"GLAD, I've found it! Something wonderful! Fulfilling and exciting. I believe that if I'd have kicked my shoes off I would have floated through the ceiling."

"What on earth are you talking about?" my wife questioned.

"Honey, I don't exactly know, but it's something new and great. Wait till I tell you . . . no, I'll have to show you."

This was my introduction to praise shortly after my salvation and deliverance from the Jehovah's Witnesses. A friend had invited me to share a trip with him, from New England, where I lived, to Atlanta, for a convention. After nearly twenty hours of nonstop driving we arrived, weary, grimy from road dust and hungry for God, but the moment we stepped into the service something was happening.

It wasn't a large gathering. Probably around 450, and being a Vermonter their exuberance startled me. They were singing with smiles on their faces, some had their hands raised, while others turned and watched us sneak in. They were singing the last verse of "How Great Thou Art," so we joined our tired voices with theirs. But at the end of the song the "Amen" was missing, when suddenly they broke into the most beautiful music I've ever heard. It was like a huge choir, and fully rehearsed. It was strange, rich, full and harmonious.

At first I couldn't make out what they were saying. Then I caught some of the words. "Hallelujah, Praise the Lord," and "Thank you Jesus." These were the words I was accustomed to, but they were using some kind of chant set to music which, apparently everyone knew except me.

After the first exhilarating moments passed the sounds softened, almost to a low hum, but the praise continued, sweet and soft. Then gently, gradually, the volume increased until the whole congregation was again lifting their voices in the realms of praise. Over and over, rolling like a great swelling tide.

At first I didn't attempt to try it, it was all so strange, and I was too conscious of my own reactions. Then I was aware that I was being lifted in my spirit, higher and higher, far beyond anything I'd ever experienced before. It seemed as though I was far beyond any of the people surrounding me. I was in God's presence and this utterly amazed me.

Generally it took prolonged waiting, agonizing prayer, and hours of Bible reading and meditation, and now in less than three minutes something happened to me that used to take hours of "waiting on God" and "praying through." That's why I excitedly exclaimed to my wife, "I found it!"

During the two days I remained at the convention I asked many questions about this practice, and learned the mechanics, but no one attempted to ground me in the Word. They simply called it "singing in the Spirit," and let it go at that. Some said it was part of "the latter day outpouring."

When I arrived back in New England I continued to ask questions. "Have you ever heard of singing in the Spirit?" For the most part the answers were, "No, why?" One man warned me against it, saying it was too emotional, but he was too late. I had already tasted and my appetite was unfulfilled. It seemed far superior to what I already had. More than that, my spirit bore witness to it, and the remarkable way it elevated me into His presence was what I had been searching for.

I found it!

IN SEARCH OF PRAISE

Endless hours of searching rabbit trails and false beginnings had long ago taught me that the quickest way to a source was to begin at the conclusion and work backwards. Revelation 19 was as near the end as I could find so I started there. It previewed the practice of the saints in Paradise.

"After these things I heard, as it were, a loud voice of a great multitude in heaven, saying, Hallelujah! Salvation and glory and power belong to our God . . . and a second time they said, Hallelujah! . . . And the twenty-four elders and the four living creatures fell down and worshiped God who sits on the throne saying, Amen. Hallelujah! And a voice came from the throne saying, Give praise to our God, all you His bond-servants, you who fear Him, the small and the great. And I heard, as it were, the voice of a great multitude and as the sound of many waters and the sound of mighty peals of thunder, saying, Hallelujah! For the Lord our God, the Almighty, reigns. Let us rejoice and be glad and give the glory to Him . . . " (Rev. 19:1-7, NAS).

There's a large crowd seen in heaven shouting "Hallelujah! Salvation and glory and power to our God." And a second time they said, "Hallelujah!" And then the twenty-four elders and the four living creatures (heavenly beings made just to worship God), fell down and worshiped the One sitting on the throne. And the wonder of it all, He exhorts them to continue.

Well, that's all right I thought. Nothing wrong with acting like that *in heaven*. But the words "loud voice" disturbed me. Perhaps it's because of their enthusiasm. After all, they had just arrived in heaven, and the excitement must have been contagious, but surely the Lord would correct that in due time. Then I read verse five, "And a voice came from the throne, saying, "Give praise to our God, all you His bond-servants, you who fear Him, the small and the great." That finished my "doing everything quietly, decently and in order" argument. It appeared that God, Himself, sanctioned their "loud" praise. My first reaction was an attempt to sidestep the issue by telling myself, that He was addressing only heavenly creatures, and not men as such. But that argument failed all too quickly when I read the words, "all you His bond-servants." Only redeemed men can be willing bond-servants. Never angels!

Obediently their voices ascended before the throne, swelling like so many waters and reverberating like the sounds of mighty peals of thunder. And not just a passing storm, but mighty peals of thunder that seemingly shook the very earth. Not a little brook tumbling downward on its way to the river but "many waters." Like the ground swells caused by tons of water pushing and being pushed by gravitational forces. Slowly lifting upward, gently cresting and then falling. Rising and falling, a mixture of height and depth, endless!

And what were they saying that sounded this way? "Hallelujah! For the Lord our God, the Almighty reigns!" Great! I agree! He does reign, but do we have to say it so loudly?

Whatever those praisers in Paradise were doing they had the Throne's approval, and I had to know not only the *what* but the *why*. The answer would be in the Scriptures.

Several facts surfaced from that one passage:

1. As a group they audibly shouted, "Hallelujah!"
2. They extolled the Lord as the Reigning King.
3. Some fell down, worshiping, by saying, "Hallelujah!"
4. All God's children, both small and great were encouraged to join in. No one was excluded from this God-given directive.
5. And finally, their combined sound was like that of an Oklahoma thunderstorm ready to spawn a dozen tornadoes.

Now, what I discovered didn't equate with anything I had observed or heard in church. Of course, I was excited and from the brief survey of praise in Paradise I knew I had to learn exactly what Biblical praise really was. What it would do—if anything—and what our current attitude towards it should be!

I soon turned to the Psalms because they consist almost entirely of praises by a number of different authors. My preliminary overview disclosed numerous exhortations to praise God! My immediate reaction was that God must either be on an ego trip, needing the praise to satisfy something in Him, or it served some purpose for us.

But God can't and doesn't change—ever—so there isn't anything about praise that benefits Him! Nothing I do or don't do changes Him! It was then I realized that since He doesn't need my praise to edify Himself, it must somehow edify me.

Just *how* would come later, but isn't that just like Him? Always providing something that increases our joy of living! Glory!

It soon became obvious that the secret—if there was one—of all the faithful men of God in the Bible was their ability to praise God when the going got tough. They weren't any different in nature, human strength or personality than we are, except, that whenever they found themselves in a tight situation they invariably cast themselves upon the Lord through praise. Somehow it lifted them out of their little world and into God's great big one.

I wanted it!

LET'S HAVE A REBELLION!

Never, in any other particular Bible study had I encountered such Satanic resistance than when I began my journey into the praise life. As soon as I set my mind with determined prayer and effort, all kinds of reactions set in. I'd become restless, or suddenly get interested in some other subject, or just plain lazy. At times I got so frustrated at the seeming magnitude of it I felt like forgetting the whole idea and just settling down with the regular Sunday morning bulletin.

I couldn't find anything written on the subject that more than scratched the surface. Nor did my commentaries help much. They all agreed that we should praise God, and assumed we did, but not one of them explained the scene I saw in Revelations 19.

Still I couldn't quit! Why would Satan resist such a simple subject, unless there was something there he didn't want me to discover? That suggestion only added to the intrigue and motivation.

Looking back I now understand why the Holy Spirit allowed this struggle. My will was involved. Our natural man must *feel* like doing something before he does it, but spiritual men submit their will *without feeling* to God. In practice, this means that we deliberately purpose to praise God. And like faith, and everything dealing with God, it springs from a confidence in the Word. It believes first, acts on that belief and feels later. Fact, faith and feeling, in that order. So you see praise doesn't always spring from my emotions, but it is triggered by an act of the will.

Without a doubt, the suggestion to raise the hands is the greatest resistance I've encountered while teaching praise. Time and time again I've watched good Christian people, for that matter meek people, become extremely hostile at the idea. It's a sore spot. Yet I've also witnessed the change in their countenance when they took that first step and obeyed God. Without exception they soon were liberated into beautiful praise.

How well I remember my first attempt at raising my hands in public. I was standing in the last pew directly against the back wall, as far from the pulpit as I could be and still be in the auditorium. Everyone else was in front of me and they weren't having any problem raising their hands. I raised my hands, about waist high, sort of held them together, and barely tapped my fingers together. (That was raising my hands and clapping them.) What an accomplishment for me! If I remember correctly, I later wiggled my toes, as my version of dancing in the Spirit. Frightened? No, I don't think so. Embarrassed? I think so! I don't believe I would have felt anymore uncomfortable had I forgotten to wear my trousers.

There's something about involving the body that brings an inner release. That's one reason why healing evangelists really work at releasing praise before they minister to the sick. It may be pride that is binding the sick, or it may be inhibitions. More than likely it's some kind of insecurity and fear. Our reasoning may be: *Is this right? Maybe it's the devil tricking me. Why hasn't my church done this before?* (There's a good chance they once did.)

Some years ago I was in Souderton, Pennsylvania, in a meeting with Gerald Derstine. We were praising the Lord one Sunday evening when a plain Mennonite lad walked in. He had a small, well-trimmed beard and a black hat. Sheepishly he slipped into the back row. After ten minutes of observing he tried the same approach I just described about myself. Trying to act casual, he barely tapped his fingers together. I can still feel his bewilderment when he saw happy folk smiling in church!

Early the next morning he stood at the front door where I was staying, all excited.

"I talked with Grandpa, last night, and told him there were some different Mennonites in town."

I smiled and waited for him to continue.

"He asked me quite a few questions about the way they sang. 'Did they shout at all, and did they smile and act happy?' Brother Trombley," he said, 'Son, maybe they're not so different after all. My ancestors settled in Souderton and we've been Mennonites for generations, and from what you're telling me, they're maybe not so different but maybe just old fashioned. I remember my Grandad telling me

13

how their camp meetings in the summer went. Sounds about the same to me.' "

So you see, perhaps your church did praise God at one time.

I was preaching an annual homecoming and camp meeting in Cape Cod, Massachussetts, some years ago, for the Advent Christian people and was teaching them along the line of charismatic gifts of the Spirit. One elderly gentleman came to me.

"Sounds to me like you've finally caught up."

"What do you mean by that?" I asked him.

"In 1850 the Advent Christian people had a sensational outpouring of the Holy Spirit right on these grounds. They praised the Lord. There was weeping, conviction and such power! Some folk lay 'slain in the spirit' for hours. But that was 1850. Hasn't been anything like it since."

And don't forget the Methodists. Along with their "methods" from which they gained their name, they were also called "Holy Rollers" due to their excessive rejoicing, falling in the spirit and power with God.

And what of the ancient Eastern Catholic Church? They used to dance and rejoice after each celebration of the Mass. Early Baptists were noted for their fervor. Yes, even the Pentecostals were quite "happy" at one time. What happened to them?

Generally it takes the second generation to forsake what the fathers appreciated, and some fought for. The desire for acceptance publically became stronger than the desire for God, and the same sick feeling that overwhelms all of us came on them. Then too, there was the fear of making a spectacle of ourselves, or offending the unsaved. For fear of "getting too much religion" we're hesitant and reluctant to release ourselves unto the Lord.

Let's have a rebellion . . . against something that really counts. Let's rebel against ourselves and demand that we fully conform to the Word of God.

In Psalm 95, which one reference called, "A Workshop on Praise," the Psalmist said, "O come, let us sing for joy to the Lord; let us shout joyfully to the rock of our salvation. Let us come before His presence with thanksgiving; let us shout joyfully to Him with psalms. . . . Come, let us worship and bow down; let us kneel before the Lord our Maker" (1, 2, 6 NAS).

How can one obey the "let us" except it be an act of his will? Rarely was the Psalmist David in circumstances that were conducive to singing, dancing, or shouting joyfully. Once when He was hiding in the deep recesses of a cave while Saul, his father-in-law king, sought to kill him, he said, "My heart is steadfast, O God, my heart is steadfast. I *WILL* sing, yes, I *WILL* sing praises!"

What's so unusual about that? Only that while he hid in the back of the cave, Saul, with murder in his heart, stood at the entrance, not knowing he was hiding there. In those conditions who feels like rejoicing? Who can sing when their mouth feels as though it were stuffed with cotton, their stomach squeezed into small knots and fear almost paralyzing them? Who? Only the man who understands and believes in the eternal loving-kindness of his God.

So David sang. Not very loudly, I'm sure, but he sang. And God heard him!

He had a way of frequently taking his feelings, as well as his intellect, by the collar and telling them to respond to the Spirit, or else. "Soul, praise the Lord!" Once he threatened to humble his soul with fasting and prayer unless it responded. It did! That's one appropriate time when you can talk to yourself.

Soon after these basic attitudes were discovered I began checking the lexicons to see if there wasn't something deeper yet. I wanted to know *how* to praise the Lord and not just *that* I should. It was during this phase of my study that I uncovered the basic or root meanings of the seven Hebrew words that are consistently translated "praise" in the Authorized Version. Consequently, it left me without a true perspective of what the Psalmist actually said and did.

Perhaps the most difficult decision a translator has to make is when to transliterate a word according to common usage, or actually render it as the root word implies. In the case of *praise* most versions simply use praise to translate these several Hebrew words so rich with meaning. This is perfectly acceptable, but I wanted a complete understanding.

IS PRAISE FOR TODAY?

In case you're questioning, as I did, whether it's applicable for New Testament believers to use the Hebrew scriptures so literally, allow me to share my discovery in answering the question.

In Psalms 102: 18-22 (NAS) I read: "Let this be written for the generation to come; that a people YET TO BE CREATED may praise the Lord. For He looked down from His holy height; from heaven the Lord gazed upon the earth, to hear the groaning of the prisoner; to set free those who were doomed to death; that men may tell of the name of the Lord in Zion, and His praise in Jerusalem; when the peoples are gathered together, and the kingdoms to serve the Lord."

Note these statements: for the generation to come, and that a people YET TO BE CREATED may praise the Lord.

Has there been another creation since Adam sinned and pulled the whole human family down into sin and death? When did God look down and bring deliverance to the prisoner? Was there another people created before the new birth at Pentecost? None that I know of.

Therefore, He must have been speaking of the *new creation,* a *new generation* that would be created when redemption was completed. This didn't take place until after Calvary and the empty tomb. Those people would praise the Lord!

By implication these people *will* praise the Lord because their deliverance is total. Take time and read Luke 4:18 and note the similarity of the passages.

IT TAKES THE SPIRIT

In Isaiah 61:1, 3 (NAS) the prophet said: "The Spirit of the Lord is upon me because the Lord has anointed me . . . to grant those who mourn in Zion, giving them a garland instead of ashes, the oil of gladness instead of mourning, the mantel of praise instead of a spirit of fainting." In other words, it takes the anointing of the Holy Spirit to really praise the Lord and give the mourning soul a dancing heart. Paul's words in Ephesians 5:18-19 agree. "Do not get drunk with wine, for that is dissipation, but be filled with the Spirit, speaking to one another in psalms and hymns and spiritual songs, singing and making melody with your heart to the Lord."

Now, if as Christ stated in John 7:37-39, the Spirit was not yet given because Jesus was not yet glorified, then real praise, from a GENERATION YET TO COME, and a PEOPLE YET TO BE CREATED, could not begin until after His resurrection, ascension and giving the Holy Spirit. Pentecost was that time!

On that day some 120 followers of Jesus waited expectantly for His promise. Suddenly it happened! The Spirit came, the old was put away and the new began. These people who heretofore had not praised the Lord found their hearts filled with joy. The river of praise began to flow. With other tongues they praised God and "spoke of the mighty deeds of God" (Acts 2:11).

Therefore, it is applicable for us, as New Testament believers, to look to the Psalms for guidance in learning how to release our praise to the Lord. If you're still not convinced then turn to Isaiah 43:19, 21 for additional confirmation:

17

"Behold, I will do something new, now it will spring forth; will you not be aware of it? . . . The people I formed for Myself, they will declare My praise."

Satisfied? God willed that He would create a new kind of people who would be and do something new. Namely, praise the Lord, His way. It will spring forth, flowing like a mighty river. Only those specially prepared by the Lord will be able to perform it.

Around the world, those fellowships that are experiencing a new move of the Spirit are experiencing renewal in praise and worship. Faces that were once frozen into religious patterns are smiling. There is joy in the camp and ofttimes under extreme pressures caused by their emphasis on praise. Whenever the Spirit falls on a congregation, or an individual, something happens. Instant praise breaks forth.

In Centerville, Ohio, is the oldest Baptist Church in the state. At the time of the outpouring it was 163 years old and going weakly. When we were asked to come the humorous remark was made, "There isn't anything you can do that will hurt it, so come and do what you can!"

On a Wednesday night after several fruitless services, in a back Sunday school room, a lady with cataracts on both eyes was instantly healed. While reading the writing on the distant blackboard something happened among 20 or so people present. Without any coaxing, they began to audibly praise the Lord, thanking Him and glorifying the Lord. Some were laughing, some had tears in their eyes, but without exception all were rejoicing. This was the beginning of the Centerville awakening. Praise came automatically when the Spirit came.

Chapter Two

How to Praise the Lord

There are seven words which portray the entire biblical portrait of praise. They are *YADAH*, *TOWDAH*, *HALAL*, *SHABACH*, *BARAK*, *ZAMAR* and *TEHILLAH*. Although I'm not hung up on Bible numerics, generally the number seven points toward totality, completeness and entirety.

YADAH

This is a verb with a root meaning the *extended hand*, to *throw out the hand*, therefore, *to worship with extended hand*. According to the lexicon, the opposite meaning is *to bemoan*, *the wringing of the hands*. In other words, if you refuse to lift your hands in victorious worship, you might be wringing them in whimpering defeat. *YADAH* is involved action, not passivity, but acting with your will, throwing your hands upward in power. It's corresponding actions whereby your dependence on God is put into action. For example: When Jehosaphat saw his little nation surrounded by the Moabites, Ammonites and others, he put his faith into action. Calling out the priests that accompanied the army, he stationed them *before* the army as leaders. Yet they were without weapons. What did they do? "And the Levites from the sons of the Kohathites . . . went out before the army, and to say, praise (*YADAH* is the word used here) the Lord; for his mercy endureth for ever" (2 Chronicles 20:19-21).

What did they do? They lifted their hands with all their strength. They had to; they were frightfully outnumbered, and certain defeat faced them. But in no way did their actions signify surrender to the circumstances or the enemy. Rather, it revealed their desperate yet total dependence on God to help them.

It was then the prophet among them received a word from the Lord. "You need not fight in this battle; station yourselves, stand and see the salvation of the Lord on your behalf." What happened?

When the enemy saw these holy men stationed before the army, standing there with their arms raised heavenward and just watching, confusion hit them. Almost immediately they turned against one another and victory came, and often comes to us also in the most unorthodox ways, but come it does. Glory!

I've often heard it exhorted: "What do you do when someone sticks a gun in your back? You put your hands up in surrender. So surrender to God. Put your hands up!"

That may sound encouraging, and I understand what they meant, but it always left me feeling uncomfortable. It implies that God might stick a gun, or something else, in my back, forcing me to praise Him. It's simply not true. He desires your praise, to be sure, but it must be freely offered.

I agree that He'll set you up, by establishing a situation, just as He did Jehoshaphat, in order to get you to learn how to trust Him, but that's a far cry from holding you up for praise.

I was reminded of a family illustration to teach me *YADAH* praise.

When my son was a little fellow, somewhere around twenty months, he discovered chewing gum. Being a good parent I wasn't as much concerned about his teeth—he didn't have that many yet—as I was about my clothes. That sticky mess frequently managed to hang on to the backside of my pants. It's miserable stuff to scrape off!

Anyway, the rule was, no gum! Moreover, we had a spoiler who visited occasionally and she nearly always had Chicklets in her purse. David's game was rummaging through Grandma's purse until he found them, and being an obedient son, I couldn't say or do much about it.

So when Dave spotted her coming he'd take off as fast as his little legs would propel him, his diapers somewhere between his knees and ankles. When he finally reached her, he wouldn't say a word; he'd just *YADAH*. Throw up his hands in the air as high as he could reach. And Mom? She wouldn't say a word either—didn't have to—but she communicated well enough. She'd bend down, pick him up, yet both knew exactly what the other needed.

He the gum, she the hug.

Is our Heavenly Father different? Not according to Scripture, He isn't. He doesn't really need your praise, but you need His response. So the next time you need Him why not throw your arms heavenward and let Him know it? Try it! You'll like it! That's *YADAH* praise, not vocal but the uplifted hands.

Man's hands have always been an extension of his inner nature. Agressive men often ball their hand into a fist and strike out at whatever stands in front of them. Jesus, however, blessed the little children by laying His open hands on them. He frequently ministered healing through His hands. The same hands, but their purposes so far apart. One to bless; the other to curse. Your hands can bless the Lord: "So I will bless Thee as long as I live; I will lift up my hands in Thy Name" (Ps. 63:4), or you can leave this part of God out of your life and "wring your hands in despair."

Further Scriptures tell us to "lift up your hands in the sanctuary and bless the Lord" (Ps. 134:2). Again in Psalm

21

141:2, the "lifting of the hands is counted as the evening sacrifice."

In I Timothy 2:8 Paul wrote, "I will therefore that men pray everywhere, lifting up holy hands . . ." This is the opposite of "wringing the hands in despair." It is adoration. It is expressed love. Therefore lift up the hands that are weak . . . and bless the Lord. I realize how difficult this will be for you the first time, but if you'll obey and trust the Scripture, it won't be long before you'll bless the Lord as David did—with everything within you—and you'll enjoy it.

TOWDAH

After I discovered that YADAH was practically unknown, hardly ever practiced, and yes, even forbidden in some assemblies, due, I suppose, to ignorance of the Scriptures, I surged forward, eager to find more.

The next word was TOWDAH and oddly it came from the same principal root we just discussed. Both involved the extension of the hand but somehow TOWDAH included more. It's also the modern Hebrew word for *thanksgiving* and is so used in the NAST. Properly it is an *extension of the hand in adoration, avowal or acceptance.*

By way of application it was apparent in Psalms and elsewhere that it was used for thanking God for *things not yet received* as well as for things already at hand. For example: "He who offers a sacrifice of thanksgiving honors Me; and to him who orders his way aright, I shall show the salvation of God." (Ps. 50:23).

The KJV translates TOWDAH in this passage as praise, leaving us in the dark as to what the Psalmist did. It is a sacrifice of thanksgiving and *it honors God,* but how and why? At least three things immediately surface: (1) TOWAH honors and glorifies God, (2) In order to work our "ways must be ordered aright," and (3) God guarantees His salvation and de-

22

liverance.

Now that's worth knowing about!

When *TOWDAH* is coupled with our conversation or attitude of life, which in the faith life we call "corresponding actions" or "acting on your faith," God guarantees deliverance.

How does *TOWDAH* glorify and honor God? Because it accepts His written Word as His guarantee that He'll stand behind it and make it good. In Jeremiah 1:12 He promised, "I am watching over my word to perform it"! God's Word is His will, so when the Word is known and relied upon, you can be assured of being in His will. That in itself forever settles the wavering statement, "If it be thy will, O Lord . . ." If God has said it, that is His will and He can't change!

God said exactly what He meant and meant exactly what He said. If He didn't mean what He said who can say what He did mean? And if he didn't say what He meant why didn't He say what He meant? Truth is, He said what he meant and meant what He said. Therefore, when we accept His Word and act upon it by thanking Him for the answer before we see it, it must come to pass. That is FAITH IN ACTION! And it honors God by taking Him at His Word without question, reservation, or any sense of doubt. *TOWDAH* then is a sacrifice of thanksgiving, rejoicing in something that is guaranteed by His Word, but which hasn't actually taken place yet, except by the eye of your faith.

In "ordering your ways aright" you put into both vocal and physical action your confidence that God means what He says and says what He means. "Stand still and see the salvation of the Lord" is still a valid order today. Quit trying to help Him out; quit answering your own prayers with your own strength, and cast yourself upon Him. *ACT* in both word and deed as though you know—because you already do—how it will turn out.

That is always the biblical combination, the mouth confessing, followed by actions. "The word of faith is nigh thee, even in thy mouth and in thy heart" (Rom. 10:8).

Let's use my son David again to illustrate this principal.

After his grandmother picked him up, there was the usual exchange of both dry and wet kisses from both parties, the search for gum and then the *TOWDAH*. His little arms reached out and encircled her neck. Nothing was said vocally, yet, nothing needed to be. That was all Granny needed. Later came the "I wove you" which served as the topping to a delicious dessert.

What better way is there of showing both our appreciation and confidence in His Word than the *sacrifice* of thanksgiving, or attitude of gratitude? Not just for what He has already done, and thank God there is a special kind of praise just for that, but for what He said He will do! That is real *TOWDAH*!

There have been times when I stood in great need and knew what the Word declared. I was acquainted with the Covenant and promises so my problem wasn't with the Word but with my own soulish realm, my intellect, my emotions, and my will. My intellect conspired with the other two trying to convince my inner man that I was acting foolishly. Meanwhile my emotions were being charged with everything from fear to ridicule while my will gradually built up a stiff resistance. Those rascals were conspiring against me to sell me out with questionings, unbelief, rebellion and a restless refusal to wait. What am I to do? So what did I do?

I opened my mouth and thanked God for His Word, often quoting Scriptures, yes, using them as praise until my inner man gained ascendency over my rebelling mental facilities and brought them into order. Paul called that mind the "carnal mind," the mind of the flesh in rebellion against God, and unable to be submissive to God. But Paul also said to cast down or pull down "imaginations, and every high thing that exalts itself against the knowledge of God, and bringing into

24

captivity every thought to the obedience of Christ" (2 Cor. 10:5).

There have been times when it was difficult to force my mouth to confess what I knew in my inner man was true. Then I just opened my Bible, held it up towards God with my left hand, turned my face toward Him and with my right fore-finger just pointed to the Scripture. It wasn't long before I was able to vocally thank Him and act on the given promise, and the answer always came. I'm not implying that it *has* to come immediately, and who of us wouldn't like it that way, but the answer *will* come. He said so!

TOWDAH is a sacrifice of thanksgiving, both for what God has done and what He has promised *to do*. Never should it be a routine mouthing "Thank you Jesus," or "Thank you God," but a deliberate action of your faith through vocal thanksgiving when you are fully conscious of your action.

In Jeremiah 17:26 the offerings were called the sacrifice of thanksgiving and in 33:11 we find the thank offering accepted by the Lord as a sacrifice. Also in Psalm 100:4 we are exhorted to enter into His presence with thanksgiving and into His courts with praise. Thank God we no longer have to approach Him with a lamb under one arm and a knife in the other hand, but because of the completed sacrifice of Jesus as the Lamb of God, we can approach Him with a mouth full of thanksgiving, knowing He will accept us for what Jesus has done. Hallelujah!

HALAL

Next I uncovered another primary root, *HALAL*, from which the word *Hallelujah* comes, as well as another word for praise, *TEHILLA*.

HALAL means to be *clear, to shine, to boast, show, to rave, celebrate, to be clamorously foolish*. (Now that's some word!)

25

This type of praise is perhaps the most commonly practiced expression of praise. Whenever God's children are gathered you'll hear them singing, magnifying His name, boasting of His exploits and in general extolling His greatness, which is exactly as it should be. But there's more! How many of you have done this until you were clamorously foolish?

Lord, do you really want me acting like that? Am I supposed to hang so loose, turned on and let go all at the same time that I . . . I can't act like that Lord! I'm a Vermonter!

"That isn't what it means," the Spirit said. "I deal with every man according to his temperament and yieldedness. You don't have to praise God at all if you don't want to; you get to!"

Nothing else was said or impressed, but I knew from past experiences the rest would come later, but not until I was spiritually strong enough to take it. I was somewhat relieved but still didn't have the full answer I desired. I knew that the root of the word said, "clamorously foolish," and I wouldn't rest easy until I understood the full implications. Sometime later the answer came with another illustration.

A young man shared with us about his first love. This was his first encounter with the "only girl in the whole world. What a wonderful missionary's wife she'll make." I let him talk on, his eyes beaming with excitement, or were those stars? Strange things happened though. Although he was a youthful teen-ager, his appetite was nilch—gone. At first it was interesting, that is for the first fifteen minutes. But after the second quarter hour it was laborously humorous. Then came the second half hour and I was begging for tolerance and grace, the whole bit. I needed it! Or was it him? He continued to explore the caverns of her dimples and almost drown me in the pools of her eyes. I felt like telling him to "hush!" Although it was obvious he was absolutely convinced, and wanted me to be also, that this girl was the *only one of her kind in the whole world*, I soon wondered if he was normal. He was acting clamorously foolish.

Then the word of the Lord came to me. "That is being clamorously foolish."

"Who me?" I asked.

"No, him, or so *you* think. He's convinced, so enthralled, so enthused, and overwhelmed with the love he feels in his heart he can't refrain from talking about her. That is exactly what I want your praising to be!"

Then I saw it and felt so foolish for having missed it. It isn't that we, the praisers, act foolish. It's just that those a-round us think we are! And until we're as enthused as the young lover, our testimony and praise will sound "like hollow noise and a clanging cymbal."

"Thank you, Lord; I see that!"

Witnessing also is getting so filled with love for Jesus, so enthused about Him, that we can't help telling others about Him. And that can't be learned in a soul-winning class but flows from a wellspring within.

So you see, we have His permission to boast on Him, to tell of His wonderful works, to brag on Him, to magnify Him, until those around us begin to wonder . . .

Of course, someone might think you're even maladjust-ed, but . . . is that bad in a sick society?

"But can't I just praise Him silently in my heart?"

I dare you! Go ahead! Something has to give sooner or later. It would be easier to contain a volcano in a teacup than a heart full of silent praise. Jesus said, "Out of the abundance of the heart the mouth speaks."

Suppose my wife said to me, "Chuck, tell me you love me!"

Shaking my head from side to side I refuse.

"Why won't you tell me you love me?" she pleads.

"Because it's only emotionalism," I explain kindly. "In my culture we don't act that way. My ancestors never told anyone they loved them audibly; they just loved them in their hearts."

In case you haven't figured out what happens next; it's easy. I'd have a nice silent divorce on my hands. Without any emotionalism or feeling. After all we're cultured! Ridiculous, isn't it? Yet that's exactly the way some imagine we should praise our Heavenly Father; however, it isn't the Bible way. True, you can begin by silently saying in your heart, "I appreciate you, Lord, for all you've done," but I guarantee you it won't be long before you'll have to say it audibly. So don't be afraid; God isn't nervous.

SHABACH

Having successfully arrived at a biblical understanding of *HALAL*, this one made me chuckle. Oh, the sense of humor the Spirit of God has. Surely this particular expression of praise is something special for the shy, the quiet or the timid believer. I smiled because I was just that kind of person until . . .

It's for those believers who hide in the rear of the congregation and if they ever clap their hands it's with the tips of their fingers. And dancing? Never, just their toes wiggle. Anything more than that leaves them frightfully breathless. Ask me how I know?

SHABACH means to *address in a loud tone*, *to command*, *triumph*, *glory*, *to SHOUT*!!! There it is again; noise, or at least a loud vocal expression, but I didn't say to do it, God did!

"In church, God? You've got to be kidding!"

"Truth is, Trombley, anywhere, God isn't particular."

In fact Psalm 117:1 urges: "O praise (SHABACH) the Lord, all ye nations." They haven't yet, but they will! God said so! In Psalm 63:1,3,4 we note David's thirst for the living God: "O God, thou art my God; I will seek Thee earnestly; My soul thirsts for Thee, my flesh yearns for Thee. In a dry and weary land where there is no water. Because thy loving-kindness is better than life, my lips shall praise (SHABACH) Thee. So I will bless Thee as long as I live; I will lift up my hands in Thy name."

So there you have it! There are times when loud praise, a crying out, a shout is very acceptable to God. Of course, we're dealing with principles and there are variables. Still the "shout" can be one of victory as well as one of desperation.

During an altar call in Philadelphia I prayed with a Mennonite man to receive the baptism in the Spirit. He was a quiet man whose nature and background rebelled against any public display of emotion. I prayed and nothing happened. I prayed several times more and still nothing happened. I called another brother and together we prayed and nothing happened.

I had instructed him to believe he was receiving, yield to the incoming Spirit, open his mouth and take the first step, but try as he would, nothing happened.

"What do you feel like doing?" I asked him.

"Oh, my," he said sheepishly, "No, I couldn't!"

"You couldn't what?"

"Well, sir, I feel like screaming, Praise God!" Even saying it made him blush.

"Then do it, man, do it!" I urged.

He had been kneeling quietly in front of us with his head bowed and his hands folded prayerfully. Looking up, he threw his hands into the air, and shouted as loud as he could, "Praise God!"

Instantly he was filled with the Spirit.

For him, the shout set him free, and he's been free since.

An elderly woman told me she was once so tormented by Satan that she resorted to *SHABACH* to make him flee. She said she was ironing and free-flowing thoughts, so negative and hate-filled, kept coming to her. She prayed but they remained, stronger than ever. She tried singing but they were still there. Finally, in an act of faith she went to the kitchen door and opened it.

"Satan, I charge you, leave my kitchen and leave me alone. I resist you in the name of the Lord. And don't you forget for one moment that Jesus conquered you; you've been stripped of your authority; you're God's idea of nothing, so get! Jesus is Lord! Now listen to mé while I praise Him for whipping you!" Now notice what she did. She not only rebuked Satan, she brought *HALAL* into it by exalting Jesus before him. He had no choice except to leave.

Psalm 47:1 says "Shout to God with a voice of triumph," while Psalm 35:27 says, "Let them shout for joy and be glad . . . Let the Lord be magnified."

BARAK

By now I needed something to help soothe me. Nearly everything I'd learned about quietness, reverence, dignity, and New England culture had been blown. Especially since my observations revealed that these dynamic expressions of praise took place in public, as well as private. So when I came to *BARAK* I was back on conservative ground again. It means *to kneel*, *to bless* God as an act of adoration. Negatively it could mean to curse God, or a form of treason, or blasphemy.

This word isn't as common but is rich and pregnant in meaning. It's often translated as "bless," or "bow down in worshipful attitude;" "to bless God *expecting to receive something.*" There's almost something instinctive in everyone of us that wants to bow before Him, whether in worship or prayer. Note its use in Psalm 72:12-15: "For He will deliver the needy when he cries for help, the afflicted also, and him who has no helper. He will have compassion on the poor and needy. And the lives of the needy He will save. He will rescue their life from oppression and violence; and their blood will be precious in His sight . . . Let them bless (BARAK) Him all day long."

Thank God for such a magnificent promise. He promises to deliver the needy, the afflicted, the poor and those oppressed by violence and bondage, *if they barak* (bow before Him expecting to receive) His name all day long. In other words, stop running. Cease your futile trying to help Him solve your problems. *BARAK*, kneel before Him, bless Him, stay there, and expect to receive the promise of His Word. A similar application is seen in Judges 5:2 when they sang the song of Deborah after the defeat of Sisera.

No! it isn't a begging attitude; it's an expecting attitude. And what better time to use your mouth to *TOWDAH* than this? How about giving Him some *HALAL* for His everlasting kindness? Many already bow in a prayerful attitude, but do you *EXPECT* anything to happen? You hope it will; you think it might; you guess it could, but that isn't *BARAK*. EXPECT A MIRACLE; that's the difference! All expressions of praise must be based and emanate from faith.

ZAMAR

By the time I got to word number six I could see that praise included much more than the usual Sunday bulletin with its two songs, responsive reading and an anthem. It was more than just saying, "Praise the Lord," or grabbing that smashed finger, and dancing while you shout, "Praise the Lord!" During this time of searching and learning, I asked myself a number of times, "Why have the leading seminaries and Bible schools withheld such precious truths and not taught them? And why wasn't there anything written to help others see the depth of praise and worship?"

ZAMAR means *to touch the strings*, and is used concordantly with instrumental worship. For example: Psalm 150 mentions a variety of instruments and tells us to praise with them, to *ZAMAR*, to touch the strings. When David said, "A-

wake my glory; awake harp and lyre, I will awaken the dawn!
I will give thanks to Thee, O Lord, among the peoples; I will
sing praises (ZAMAR) to Thee among the nations." He used
ZAMAR for praise. (Ps. 57:8-9).

ZAMAR praise is mostly rejoicing. Most of the instruments mentioned in Psalm 150 are either percussion or rhythm.
Lots of volume and downbeat, but they were used to rejoice
before the Lord (I Chron. 15:16).

Two years ago I held a Praise Seminar on Long Island
near the end of the year. This Christian Retreat announced
that on New Year's Eve they would put into practice what I
had been teaching. They would have an all-night praise party
where everyone would come expecting to participate with
praise, and various kinds of instruments. Each one was encouraged to do something different.

"If I were coming," I told the director, "I believe I'd
get me a 20-quart milk can, put in a shovelful of crushed
stone and come shaking it for the glory of God."

"Do you have Scripture for that?" he asked.

"Believe I do. Jesus told the Pharisees that if they
wouldn't praise Him the very rocks around them would cry
out. He didn't say exactly how, so I'll use my sanctified imag-
ination and do it my way. I'll bring a bucket and shake it for
Jesus." We both had a good chuckle, but I had a greater one
some weeks later when he called.

"Chuck, we have our praise party. Do you remember
my telling you that we needed $30,000 the next day, New
Year's Day, for the down payment for this property? We just
didn't have it so we committed it to the Lord. Anyway, we
had a full house. All night we praised the Lord, sang and
shouted. Next morning Brother _____ from Massachu-
setts called and asked me if we needed $30,000." I had to
patiently wait while he quieted down his shouting.

"He said the Lord told him that we needed that a-
mount!"

Not once was that amount mentioned publically, nor was the burden passed to someone else. The director simply laid it before the Lord and had the praise party. They put *ZAMAR* into full orbit, and Jesus met the need. After all, with so few folk willing to give Him full praise, He wasn't about to let some that did go broke and default, was He?

Later the director's wife was healed from advanced, terminal cancer the same way!

TEHILLAH

Finally, I arrived at word number seven. A word that means simply to *sing*, to *laud*. Now all singing is praise and God's children are noted for their singing, but *TEHILLAH* is singing our *HALAL*. Then I uncovered something that really sent me searching. In Psalm 22:3 I read that "God inhabits or is enthroned in the praises of His people." We've all known that but did you know the word for praises here is plural of *TEHILLAH*? In this particular kind of praise He manifests Himself. But is God always manifested in just singing?

"Lord, in that little, indifferent church where I grew up . . . did you manifest yourself there when they sang?"

"No, He informed me, "they didn't really care whether I was there or not."

"Well, Lord, we used to sing in the Kingdom Hall. Were you there?"

"Sorry, son, they didn't even know who I was."

"How about the Pentecostal churches, Lord. I've visited them and how they sing. Were you there?"

"Not always. When their singing came from their hearts and was directed towards Me I was there, but they have a tendency to take Me for granted."

Interesting, I thought. And what is there to prevent me from falling into the same rut? I realized that even our fellowship with the Father could suffer from the same doldrums that affect too many marriages, that of taking one another for granted. Praise and worship, like a good marriage relationship, must be worked at, preserved and guarded from this pitfall.

So there is singing . . . and there is singing.

More than 300 times in Scripture we are exhorted to sing with some eight different Hebrew words for sing, among them shout, a shrill sound, gladness and strolling minstrel. One thing is common in them; they are all joyful and triumphant. A release of the emotions. But isn't that bad? Not when you know it's the best health remedy available. "A merry heart maketh good like a medicine."

Singing has always been a traditional part of Christian worship. Nearly every service, regardless of the communion where it is practiced, begins with singing. The early martyrs established their testimony by singing praise while they slowly marched to their sure death at the pleasure of the hungry lions in pagan Rome. During the great war many in German concentration camps astonished their captors with their joyful singing. Slaves chopped cotton while singing spirituals; mothers sang at the funerals of their children and businessmen while watching their fortunes vanish. No, it wasn't nervous singing but rejoicing in the Lord, an expressed confidence, an inner joy that the world doesn't possess, much less understand.

Further study revealed that psalms, hymns and odes were singing and could be praise and yet not be *TEHILLAH* which was where God dwelt. This came to light in 2 Chronicles 20:22.

When Israel began to sing *and* to praise *(TEHILLAH)*, the Lord sent ambushments against her enemies. If *TEHILLAH* was ordinary singing and not some special kind of singing, then why did the text say both sing and *TEHILLAH?* Two different words are used because two different expressions are meant. It was then my research led me to Ephesians

5:18-19: ". . . be filled with the spirit, speaking to one another in psalms, hymns and spiritual songs . . ."

There it was—spiritual songs—a song which is a manifestation of the indwelling Spirit as any other manifestation of the Spirit (1 Cor. 12:7). Prophecy is the outflowing of the Spirit from within the believer. Tongues flow forth from the selfsame Spirit as does knowledge, wisdom, teaching or giving. It is a manifestation of the indwelling Spirit of God. So this *TEHILLAH* singing wasn't just spirited singing, but actual songs of the spirit, unprepared, unpremeditated, often unlearned, that flowed forth as a result of being filled with the Spirit.

Was this what I head in Atlanta? Was this "flowing in praise" what David taught the priests when he taught them to sing by course? (1 Chronicles 15:16-22).

Both instruments and singers were to raise "sounds of joy," which in the Hebrew means "bright, merry." In verse 17 some were appointed who would praise the Lord in the first rank. Next came those from the second rank (v. 18). The text implies a degree, a copy, a double, so a degree of ascent. This was harmony based on the music scale.

Then in verse 20 there were those who had their harps tuned to *alamoth* which in the original means "maiden-like tone." In other words the soprano tone, while the next verse the lyres were tuned to the *sheminith* which is the octave or 8th note. It was eight notes below the *alamoth,* or soprano. We'd call it the bass. So what did they have? Full harmony using both voices and instruments.

Any form of singing can be praise, but the highest was the Dorean mode which was neither western major nor oriental minor. It was a sort of chanting whereby the words of *HALAL* were melodiously chanted. It was THIS expression of praise that the Psalmist said God inhabited. It was THIS expression of praise that brought about the defeat of Israel's enemies as the priests stood before them. It is THIS expression of praise that ushers us into His court (Ps. 100:4). It is THIS expression of praise, today called "singing in the spirit," that is unifying the Body of Christ. From all I've concluded it is THIS climax of praise that the other forms of praise lead up to.

Somehow I saw the first six forms of praise much like a pilot making an airplane fly. The aircraft, left to itself, can't and doesn't fly. The pilot causes it to fly. As long as it sits on the parking lot, or in the middle of the runway, nothing happens. But let's do something.

Point the nose down the center of the runway, get clearance from the tower, and gradually force the throttle to the firewall and hang on. For a few moments the plane still doesn't fly but we're gradually changing that mode. It's picking up speed as it charges down the strip.

Soon a critical speed is reached where certain aerodynamic laws take over, and the wing and the elevator surfaces begin to float on a surface of air. It's then the plane is lifted from the ground and begins to fly.

What happened is this! Brute force, many horsepowers of it, either piston or jet, plus skill and time are involved until flying speed is reached. The ship is pulled or pushed through the air until a higher law than the law of gravity takes over. In fact, until the plane reaches a safe cruising altitude this mechanical force is fully maintained. Then much of this brute force can be cut back.

If the plane is designed correctly, for example, a sailplane, when proper altitude is achieved, the mechanical force can be completely cut free, and the plane enters free flight. The pilot, mimicking the bird, tests the air currents and floats on them. As long as he stays in that air flow he will stay aloft. Get out of it and he's headed for home.

This is exactly how praise works.

We come into His presence with thanksgiving, praise, shouting, hand clapping, loud singing, whatever. We're getting the Lord's ship, his people, ready for takeoff. Now don't get super-spiritual with me and say you're different; you're not! You're human, aren't you? It's this deliberate joyful praise that is designed to lift you into His presence, away from the normal and abnormal cares of life, the pressures on the ground, the problems you've confronted; where we can enter into and enjoy true worship in the spirit, *TEHILLAH*.

It's there, in His presence, that we find healing, deliverance, answers to prayers, relaxation (this is the rest and refreshing Isaiah told about in 28:11,12), fellowship with Him and one another, unity, strength and so much more.

But what frequently happens is this. We get the church barely off the runway, just begin to actually fly and headed for free flight in the Spirit, when hardly before the wheels are off the ground, we throttle back and give the announcements. Later we wonder what happened. Someone quenched the Spirit; that's what happened! Church—take off, soar into the heavenlies with Him and STAY THERE until you've learned what true praise and worship is!

In 2 Chronicles 5 there's the account of the dedication of the first temple. One hundred twenty priests were appointed to blow the trumpets while "in unison the trumpeters and the singers were to make themselves heard with one voice of praise (Halal—to cast up, extol) and to glorify the Lord, and when they lifted up their voice, accompanied by trumpets, cymbals and instruments of music, and when they praised the Lord saying, 'He indeed is good for His loving-kindness is everlasting,' then the house, the house of the Lord, was filled with a cloud, so that the priests could not minister because of the cloud, for the glory of the Lord filled the house of God" (12-14).

When God and man get together, the glory fills the house. When their praise extolled, cast Him up and exalted Him, then His glory filled them.

Since those early days I've happily discovered that Paul

mentions another aspect of praise which is strictly New Testament inasmuch as the Holy Spirit baptism wasn't given in the previous dispensation. "The Holy Spirit was not yet given because Jesus was not yet glorified" (John 7:39). That, of course, referred to what began at Pentecost and has continued since. So Paul mentions a praise in I Corinthians 14:15 which he calls "singing with the Spirit." It's a high form of thanksgiving, a blessing with the Spirit, a giving of thanks (see verses 16,17), which, when sung, becomes the spiritual songs of Ephesians 5:18, and is extremely edifying.

By the time I had these seven words researched—and the New Testament cousins—both from their root meanings and spiritual applications, and in the process of adapting them into my spiritual walk, I experienced what we already know. Change doesn't come easily for any of us. Habits, long established in both heart and mind, tend to hang on long after a better way is found.

For example: the diet for the overweight. They know they should lose weight so they study a proper diet which usually includes a drastic change in eating habits, adding certain foods and eliminating others. Is it easy? Ask most anyone who has tried it!

And praise was to be no different. It took some quality decisions on my part, but it was worth it! I could come to no other conclusion except that praise, if done the Biblical way, was vocal, extremely expressive, forcible at times, and had to be acted upon, all that is expected in *TEHILLAH*. That was a standing still, a coming to the end of your efforts, an entering into, a lifting up which resulted in a flowing forth. No struggle, just a flowing forth. Little wonder it was the ultimate that all other praise led into.

Chapter Three

The Praise of Sacrifice

The Bible teaching on the SACRIFICE OF PRAISE is often confused with the PRAISE OF SACRIFICE. Both are praise but from two different perspectives. One is the praise of thanksgiving, offered in spite of circumstances, regardless of natural evidence, or of the denial by our senses. It is the rejoicing for the promises in the Word.

ACCEPTANCE

The PRAISE OF SACRIFICE, however, is altogether different. Both are precious in the sight of God, both are necessary, both are acceptable and both are scriptural. The PRAISE OF SACRIFICE usually costs us MORE. David said to Ornan, "I will not offer an offering that costs me nothing" (I Chron. 21:24). This praise comes in the midst of conflict when there seems to be no apparent reason for the battle. It springs into a simple, childlike trust in God who is in charge and is doing what is best. It is a sacrifice laid at His feet, an offering to Him of something which we love, something precious to us.

It is the joyful acceptance of the messed up present as part of God's natural plan for my future. "For I know the plans I have for you, says the Lord. They are plans for good and not for evil, to give you a future and a hope" (Jer. 29:11).

Paul said, "And we know that God causes all things to work together for good to those who love God, to those who are called according to His purpose" (Rom. 8:28).

When Israel was forced, led into the wilderness, it wasn't that God intended them to suffer beyond their endurance. According to Deuteronomy 6:1,2,24 it was for their good. God wanted to humble them, test them, in order to let them know what was in their hearts, whether they would obey Him or not. It may sound cruel but it wasn't. He later promised them blessings beyond their grandest dreams (see Deuteronomy 28:1-14). But the methods He used were "far out." He included everything from hunger to hornets; from lack of water to sustained clothing supplies. The Lord directly intervened. To Israel He made known *His ways,* but *His acts* He revealed to Moses. Those in the conflict knew something was happening but only Moses understood why.

God has a plan for our lives, but He can't move us into it unless we're willing. That's what James (1:2-3) meant when he wrote, "Consider it all joy, my brethren, when you encounter various trials, knowing that the testing of your faith produces endurance." Likewise, Peter said, "In this you greatly rejoice, even though now for a little while, if necessary, you have been distressed by various trials, that the proof of your faith, being more precious than gold which is perishable, even though tested by fire, may be found to result IN PRAISE AND GLORY, and honor at the revelation of Jesus Christ" (1 Pet. 1:6,7).

So it is out of *this* aspect of praise that we should accept from God everything in our lives that involves the trial of our faith. Rather than pleading with Him to change the circumstances, this praise will result in further praise and glory to God. This is praising God *FOR* what He *IS* rather than what He has *DONE!* It is an acceptance of God's justice, mercy and goodness when I'm in a place where I can't see my way out and don't understand His silence.

40

It's like the drowning victim struggling with his rescuer. Only when he allows himself to relax, accept his present circumstance, can someone stronger rescue him. Anything less and he will drown.

It is *not* thanking God for evil, sin, rebellion and the like; it is an acceptance of the trial of our faith for His purposed glory.

AN OFFERING

Throughout Israel's history both sacrifices and offerings were part of her fellowship with God. Yes, there was praise, worship, unspeakable joy and rejoicing; but there were also sacrifices and offerings made unto the Lord. Let's not lose sight of this important fact in understanding the place of praise in the faith walk.

It costs something! It is dear to one's heart, this PRAISE OF SACRIFICE. It is giving over to God what seemingly is my personal happiness, health, wealth, life and future. My struggling ceases and I turn it over to Him without knowing the outcome because I don't know the cause. It is trust expressed as a PRAISE OF SACRIFICE.

When Hannah gave her long-awaited son back to God it was a worship and praise sacrifice. It cost her something. She had waited and longed for many years. When the Lord finally granted her a child in her old age, she immediately gave him back to God as His servant. She visited him at the temple and rejoiced that her only begotten was in continual rejoicing before the Lord. Thus Samuel, the prophet, was born and what a fellowship he had with God!

Job was declared by God to be a "righteous man, who hated evil and craved goodness." The Lord, however, gave Satan direct permission to strip him of his family, wealth and health, man's three most precious possessions.

It wasn't long before his children were abducted by enemy armies. His wealth dissipated overnight when marauders

41

plundered everything he possessed. Then his health vanished when his body was covered with boils. Even his wife doubted his sanity and suggested "he curse God and die." Yet the Word records, he "fell down on the ground, and worshipped, saying, the Lord gave, and the Lord taketh away; blessed by the name of the Lord."

He didn't fight God, but accepted his situation. He thanked God for his former provision and prosperity, and thanked God for his present poverty. He blessed the name of the Lord regardless of his painful present.

No, I don't find any evidence Job ever thanked God for his boils, or his loveless friends. Nor do I find him questioning God's dealings in his problem. What he did do was accept and trust, saying, "even though God slay me yet I will trust Him" (Job 13:15).

And what of David? How he fasted and prayed for his little son's life but God said, "No!" and the boy died. In spite of this he entered into the house of the Lord, David's tabernacle, and worshipped (see 2 Samuel 12-15-20). Did he question the Lord's ways? Again I find no evidence of this in Scripture.

When we can offer the PRAISE OF SACRIFICE for His ways, even when they seemingly contradict our ways and our understanding of the Word, that is the PRAISE OF SACRIFICE.

Moses knew God and had a "face-to-face" relationship with him but in Exodus 4 he argued with God about his venture to Egypt to deliver the enslaved Israelites. He reminded God about his speech impediment. For the past forty years he dwelt on the backside of the desert, tending sheep for his father-in-law. He was in defeat and fearful because forty years previous he murdered an Egyptian and was wanted for murder. Now at the age of 80 he was tongue-tied.

Then Moses said to the Lord, "Please, Lord . . . I am slow of speech, and slow of tongue. Isn't there someone else you can send?"

I would have expected the Lord to instantly loose his stammering tongue, put a tiger in his defeated tank, and ship him off as the mighty man of power. Instead God said, "Who has made man's mouth? Or who makes him dumb and deaf, or seeing or blind? Is it not I, the Lord? Now then go, and I, even I, will be with your mouth and teach you what you are to say" (Exod. 4:10-12).

The first time I read that it completely stumped me. Please don't write and ask me to explain it, I can't! I just accept it. I know from the Word that God is against sin, sicknesses, infirmities, and has provided total deliverance from them, but here is a situation where He acknowledged Moses' petition but refused to rectify it. Why, I don't know, except that as God He knew exactly what He could do with and through Moses. What is remarkable is Moses' attitude. He obeyed.

And what of Abraham's son? This is the classic example of the PRAISE OF SACRIFICE in the Word. After twenty-five long years of waiting while his age crept from 75 towards 100, he kept the promise of a son hidden in his heart. Now at 100, the son of promise is born. Talk about a sacrifice costing something, God called him the "Darling of his heart."

But the day came when Abraham was about 110 and God said, "Take now thy son, thine only son Isaac, whom thou lovest . . . and offer him there for a burnt offering" (Gen. 22:2).

Little wonder Abraham is called the father of the faithful. Listen to his response: "I and the lad will go yonder and worship" (Gen. 22:5). I can't imagine how he felt, or what must have been going through his mind. I'm sure I would probably have rebuked the devil, in Jesus' name, of course. The difference was, Abraham knew the voice of God and didn't quibble with Him. Turning to his servants he said, "Wait here, while I and the lad go yonder and sacrifice."

This is the PRAISE OF SACRIFICE. It costs something.

43

It is willingly offered, not knowing the reason behind it.

As you make this sacrifice to the Lord you'll enter into a new realm of praise. It may hurt, it may break you, yes, it may crush you, but remember, "The sacrifices of God are a broken spirit: a broken and contrite heart, O God, thou wilt not despise" (Ps. 51:17).

The PRAISE OF SACRIFICE is *not* passively submitting to the unknown, but an active entering into the will and purpose of God for your life. A will perhaps, at that time you don't comprehend. All you know is He loves you and knows what you have need of.

Job was harassed by Satan because God knew the independence and self-love so deeply entrenched in his personality that he wasn't aware of. (See Job chapters 27 and 29.) After his horrible trial, he was delivered, restored and came out of the conflict a better man.

Certainly Peter was a man of God, personally chosen by Jesus as one of His twelve, yet Jesus gave Satan special permission to "sift him as wheat" (Luke 22:31-32). Why would a Lord that loved him pull a stunt like that? Because He *did* love him. Jesus saw something in Peter that only a severe trial could expose. Peter's cocksure attitude of never failing would trip him from his pinnacle into the pit of denial (v.34). Jesus loved him and knew the outcome beforehand. So Peter, when the trial came, submitted and accepted (v. 32). Later he understood why but not at the time of the trial.

The PRAISE OF SACRIFICE functions in a different realm than the SACRIFICE OF PRAISE. It will bring healing but healing isn't the principal issue. It brings deliverance but the question isn't deliverance. It's "What's going on Lord?" The concern of this PRAISE is the acceptance of the question of God's plan for my life.

Battles will come, the Word promises them, but when they do, and I can't seem to operate my faith, then I'll trust Him with the PRAISE OF SACRIFICE. I'll thank Him without understanding what it's all about.

Recently my brand new daughter-in-law called with her husband from New Orleans. For some months she has suffered severe pains in her abdomen. The day before her wedding she had a thorough examination and the doctor said, "I can't find anything wrong with her. There isn't anything organically wrong. I just don't know!" Yet the pain was real, at times almost squeezing the breath from her.

"Dad," my son said, "something has to give with Margaret. She's suffering terribly and the doctor said there isn't anything organically wrong with her. What do you think it is?"

I could have been super-spiritual and blamed everything from demons to nerves, but frankly I didn't know. When I performed their marriage I didn't discern any spirits. What could I do but pray?

"Dave, let's thank God for her. I don't understand what He's doing in all this, but rest assured He's doing it. We've prayed for her healing while we were there. It should be gone, but it isn't! Let's offer the PRAISE OF SACRIFICE!"

We praised, prayed and then praised again, rejoicing in His faithfulness. Several times I said, "Because of Thy loving-kindness Lord, we trust You. I set this girl in your presence and care."

No, this wasn't a negative confession; neither was it abandoning my faith in His Word. I was up against a trial that wasn't responding normally so I simply dumped it into His hands. I suggested that she just thank the Lord for His goodness, expecting Him to care for her. We didn't praise Him specifically for her healing, nor did we praise Him except that He is the Lord whose mercy is everlasting.

About an hour later my son called back. Said he got out his guitar after he hung up and sang some praises. Then read the Bible to her for some little time, when suddenly the pain vanished. God came into the situation. Who can understand it? We simply trust Him!

Over the years I've found it difficult to minister to those who suffer from insomnia, until I discovered the PRAISE OF SACRIFICE.

I was called to pray for a lady in Sarasota, Florida, some years ago, suffering from insomnia. No amount of drugs or therapy relaxed her enough to enter into a restful sleep. Fear and pain were deeply etched in the lines bordering her tired face.

"I'm so tired," she whimpered with tears in her eyes. Her doctor brother stood by her side. "Isn't there anything that can be done?" he pleaded. "Medicine is ineffective."

Her husband informed me that only after days of near total exhaustion would she fall asleep, but after a few short hours would awaken, usually with a dreadful headache.

Only after sharing with her (the tension was undoubtedly satanic in origin and would be released when she released it to the Lord) did we begin to minister to her. Then a revelation came after we had been praying, almost fruitlessly for some time.

"It's being made clear, now, that the Lord IS dealing with you and has been. You've resisted His leading, consequently this tension is killing you. I believe it concerns your changing your work habits. Yes, I believe it's a new venture your husband and you are getting ready to undertake. If you're ready to say, 'Lord, we accept what you've been doing in my life and health for all these months,' there will come a sudden release."

"Well, we have been uncertain. My husband wants to go into a new business and he believes the Lord is leading that way, but I've been so skittish about it. It will mean the loss of our security, home and who knows what? Do you suppose this has something to do with that?"

"Are you ready to say, 'Lord I accept what is happening in my life as being permitted by You and is for my best. I thank you for it?' "

She did, her husband did, and within days she was sleeping soundly for the first time in many months. And their new business prospered.

What happened?

ONLY when she stopped her struggling, stopped fighting His ways in her life, and thanked God for them, was she delivered. She offered to Him the PRAISE OF SACRIFICE in total trust in His all sufficient love.

In Christian life, tests, trials and seemingly insurmountable circumstances, rather than being mere satanic stratagems of defeat, are stimulation opportunities in which your praise-faith-experience can glorify God. The PRAISE OF SACRIFICE is graciously accepting from your Heavenly Father all those encounters. Don't allow your heart to become calloused and bitter, uncaring, questioning God's Word and faithfulness. He knows exactly what is needed for your spiritual development. We may or may not comprehend what or why He's doing it, but we do trust Him and recognize it as good. Memorize Romans 8:28 until it becomes part of your inner man and then offer to Him your thanksgiving.

So all the paths of God are the paths of praise.

Now let's take that journey into the PRAISE OF SACRIFICE.

Chapter Four

Is It Necessary?

"But Thou art holy, O thou that inhabitest the praises of Israel" (Ps. 22:3 KJV), "And David and all Israel went up to Baalah, that is, Kirjah-jearim, which belongs to Judah, to bring up from there the ark of God, the Lord who is enthroned above the cherubim, where His name is called" (I Chron. 13:6 NAS).

Even though the throne of God is the heart of His creation, He has particularly chosen to enthrone Himself on the praises of His people. If there were no other exhortations to praise, no other benefits that could be realized, this one alone would suffice. We were created for praise; it being the grandest, greatest work a child of God can do; the highest expression he can show!

Scripture reveals that the eternal God "dwells between the cherubim" and "inhabits the praises of Israel." Does this mean that He has confined Himself exclusively to these two mediums? Hardly, since David said that wherever we went the Lord was there (Ps. 139:7-9). Being omnipresent (everywhere present) in the universe, His life flows out and touches every living thing. "In Him we live, and move, and have our being" (Acts 17:28). Yet the Word declares that as far as earth is concerned, His direct manifestation and power are evident only when His people recognize Him as the reigning Lord and provide Him with an atmosphere of joyful praise. *Yashab* means to inhabit, sit down, dwell, to settle down, where He lives.

Signs, miracles and wonders accompany His praise. Healings are manifested where praise is offered. Jesus commended the leper who returned to thank Him for the visible healing in his life. The other nine? No one really knows whether they acknowledged their healing or not. When Israel rejoiced, both before and after their trials, God made Himself strong on their behalf.

It isn't that He must have the praise before He can work. He is able to do whatever He desires, with or without us. It's His desire, as a loving Father, to minister unto us, but He's conditioned those blessings on our acknowledgment and acceptance of His Lordship. Praise is for us.

Our problem isn't with our circumstances but with our unbelief, doubts and inner rebellions. Praise, biblical praise, according to the Word, will overcome those doubts, strengthen the Word in you and increase your faith, thereby pleasing God. "And without faith it is impossible to please him. For he who comes to God must believe that He is, and that He is a rewarder of those who seek Him" (Heb. 11:6 NAS).

Therefore, there is a vital link between the Ark of the Covenant and praise God inhabits, manifests Himself, enthrones Himself in them. One is where He is; the other what we do there.

When David returned the Ark of the Covenant, also called the Ark of Strength, to Jerusalem, he set up a tent to house it and appointed some 4,000 priests to stand before it and play their instruments and praise the Lord. And this is no three-minute anthem. The priests are "to stand every morning to thank and to praise the Lord, and likewise at evening" (I Chron. 23:5, 30). "And appointed some of the Levites as ministers before the ark of the Lord, even to celebrate and to thank and praise the Lord God of Israel" (I Chron. 16:4). And oh, my! "Priests blew trumpets continually before the ark of the covenant of God" (I Chron. 16:6). Day and night, without letup shifts of priests stood and praised the Lord. Wonder what the neighbors thought of that? At 2 A.M. yet? Wherever the Ark was, there was praise!

But it wasn't always like that.

In all matters relating to worship, the tabernacle, the furniture, sacrifices or the priesthood, detailed instructions were given in the book of Exodus and they had to be followed to the letter. Nothing could be added or subtracted under the circumstances. Yet many years later we find David making changes in the priesthood and their order of service. Rather than sacrificing animals they now offered only praise. And not just a few were involved. He appointed a great number and instructed them how they were to praise the Lord. And amazing though it is, the added change wasn't rejected and judged by God but accepted.

If you recall your Bible, no one acted carelessly before the things of God. Anyone offering "strange fire" or "false sacrifices" was put to death. Even when David brought the ark back Uzzah was smitten to death for merely touching it. He didn't do it rebelliously. They were using a clumsy ox cart to transport the Ark and it began to fall. Almost without thought Uzzah reached out to steady it, but it wasn't in accordance with divine instructions. So when David arranged the people in praising God, no fire fell from heaven to consume them. Neither were they smitten; in fact, God accepted it with great pleasure, establishing the fact that praise is acceptable to Him. Even when former methods are violated and replaced by it. Prayer can be abominable; sacrifices can be abominable, but praise? Never is praise rejected by God.

During the twenty years and seven months the Ark was missing, which included the reign of Saul, there was no recorded praise in Israel. It was during that time that the tabernacle of Moses, still at Gibeon, continued business as usual (I Chron. 16:39). Their rites were maintained, they sacrificed animals, the priests washed themselves as always, they faithfully changed the oil and trimmed the wicks on the lamps, and the bread of the presence was renewed daily. Everything was normal except the Ark. It was missing! The glory had departed, the light was gone; God's voice was silent; He was gone!

So when it came time to sprinkle the blood; when it came time for atonement; when it was time to inquire of the Lord, they didn't. They couldn't! The Ark was missing! But being humans they did the best with what they had, so they learned to get along without it until, finally, they grew accustomed to "doing without the Ark," and the praise that accompanied it.

We know this to be so because when the Philistines returned the Ark after having held it for a period of seven months, the Israelites left it at the house of Abinadab in Kirjath-jearim, and left it there for twenty more years. Now it seems rational to me that if they had really missed the Ark and God's presence they would have moved that thing back to Gibeon at double speed, but they didn't. I find no evidence they even missed it, so why didn't the prophet Samuel see that it was returned? According to I Samuel 7:3, it was because of their foreign gods, their substituted religious practices, which seemingly satisfied them.

Human nature demands worship. It's created into them and if they won't worship the true Lord in truth they'll soon substitute what they think is truth and then call it truth! So how long did Israel refuse to repent and clear away their artificial lords? Twenty years! Think of it! Twenty years without the Covenant blessings. Twenty years without God making Himself known in their presence.

The Ark was missing, and so was the glory of God. Because the Ark and praise were absent so was His manifest presence and power. No wonder Israel lost her battles during those "dark ages." Little wonder Saul was such a sorry king

51

and spiritual leader. Later when David succeeded him he said, "Let us bring again the ark of our God to us; for we inquired not at it in the days of Saul" (I Chron. 13:3). When both the Ark and praise are gone all that is left is an empty ceremony. God stayed with the Ark wherever it went.

During the seven months the Philistines had it, they encountered one continual manifestation of God's power among them. During the twenty years Abinadab housed it he was blessed beyond his wildest imaginations. Where the Covenant is, there God is and where the Covenant is, there the promises are. So if God is where the Ark is then I personally want to know where it is today.

Church history reveals that the early church had both the presence and power of the living Christ among them. The church had the Ark and the glory of God but somehow lost them!

What happened?

Shortly after the Lord's ascension, men began to establish themselves in place of His presence. The spiritual power displayed in the Book of Acts was soon dispensationalized into "yesterday" and "not for today." Gradually, ceremony, rituals, bondages and ungodliness gutted the church and the Ark was misplaced. Organizational structures and an earthly human throne governed by men, in the name of the Lord, of course, were substituted for the true Ark, the place of praise. Services, rather than being a time of rejoicing, joyful singing, dancing and shouting, became as quiet as Moses' tabernacle. And for the same reason, the Glory had departed.

Is this true? Let Jesus answer for Himself.

He said in Revelation, chapters 2 and 3, that false apostles (false because they lacked the true signs and power of an apostle) had set themselves in control of His body replacing both Him and the Spirit of God. They became known, Jesus said, as "Nicolaitans," which in the Greek means, "conquering the laity." He also said, "The Gentiles exercise Lordship over one another but it shall not once be named among you." Now this was where "Satan's throne is" and where "Satan dwells" (Rev. 2:13). This new system finally matured to the place where their control was so absolute that they taught God's people how to eat "things" offered to images and statues. No longer were they questioned; their authority was absolute. Like Saul, they stood head and shoulders above the people.

If the Ark and praise were where God was enthroned, then the absence of the Ark and praise is where Satan's throne is. It has to be! Jesus wasn't speaking of some pagan temple down the road, but His church, where He was the Messenger; where He was supposed to be the Head and where there were some dear saints still serving Him. His church was where Satan's throne was. It was the substitute.

This is a sad commentary, a portrait of what men, without the Ark or His Lordship, can do to God's people. We criticize Israel for her foolish actions while we follow the same trail.

So the church forsook the true Ark and the absolute Lordship of Jesus and ended up with something God called, "wretched, miserable, poor, blind, naked and lukewarm." Something He would spit out of His mouth as sickening (Rev. 3:16-19).

Again the Ark was missing!

Again God would raise up another David to restore it. Rather this time it will be one of David's sons.

During King David's early reign he purposed to bring the Ark again. And he did! Likewise during this time of need God has promised to restore the Ark again. How can we be so sure? Turn to Acts 15:15-17: "After these things I will return, and I will rebuild the tabernacle of David which has fallen, and I will rebuild its ruins, and I will restore it, in order that the rest of mankind may seek the Lord, and all the Gentiles who are called by my name." This is a direct quote from Amos 9:11, so from the mouth of two or more witnesses every truth is established.

There are several pertinent facts in this prophecy. We won't be able to touch them all, but I trust it will quicken your understanding.

1. This will take place *in the last days.*

2. *I will return.* No human will be used this time but Jesus, the greater David, who will rebuild the tabernacle Himself. This, of course, fulfills the covenant oath Jehovah made with David in I Chronicles 17:10-14, wherein he was promised a seed to sit on his throne, and the house for the Lord he desired to build will be built by his seed, Jesus.

Can you think of one or more persons God used to bring forth the current restoration? I can't because there are none! This is strictly the work of the Lord. Were it not, it would, like most other visitations, be confined strictly to one particular segment of the church. Instead the Spirit is being outpoured on the whole Body with such magnitude it can't be withstood. Glory!

3. I will *rebuild,* signifying, not church renewal, but RESTORATION of something that is in complete shambles.

4. What is being restored? David's Tabernacle. Not Solomon's temple; not Herod's temple; not the Antichrist's temple; but David's tabernacle.

5. I will *restore* it. Precious little remains of it but the promise is, complete restoration as in the days of old. All that the tabernacle contained was the Ark of the Covenant, but that was God's dwelling place, His earthly throne, the place of fellowship between He and man, that He is restoring.

6. And whatever this restoration is it will result in multitudes of unsaved people seeking the Lord.

7. Finally, revival among even those Gentile nations who are called by His name. When Amos and years later, James, verbalized this prophecy there weren't any Gentile nations called by the name of the Lord, but today there are many.

Nations calling themselves Christian but lacking the biblical trademark of believers. This tells me, at least, that I can expect some type of national revival among the nations calling themselves Christian, but like the Laodiceans don't recognize their need.

So Jesus stands as John saw Him, on the outside looking in and knocking. Meanwhile, the church rejects Him, saying, "Leave us alone. We don't need change or restoration; we only need to perfect that which we have." But He continues knocking and He'll gain an entrance, slowly but surely.

How? Through people who have encountered Him at the Ark, and through praise. He said, "I will rebuild, I will restore," and who can withstand Him for long? So people are being filled with the Spirit; Christ is being enthroned in their lives; they're grinning instead of growling; and they're infecting the rest of the Body. The Ark is being restored and returned.

In passing, please note that the Ark involves praise.

Even when Israel rejected and abandoned it, God maintained His purpose and desire. "And David went up, and all Israel, to Baalah, that is, to Kirjath-jearim, which belongs to Judah, to bring up the ark of God the Lord, that dwelleth between the cherubims, where his name is called" (I Chron. 13:6).

Kirjath-jearim is close to Zion, the city of God. This city was in Judah which means "praise." Interesting also is the fact that Jesus, the son of David, came from Judah. The Ark today is Jesus praise.

Why leave the Ark in a strange place any longer due to neglect or ignorance? You can have a new beginning! Go get the Ark! It's all a matter of desire and will. While the current restoration is great, we haven't seen the full restoration of the Tabernacle, but of this I'm sure, the Ark is in Judah, praise. And that's why this message is being restored to the Body.

It was at Ekron when the Philistines, being heathen, realized that the Ark was a problem to them. It was offensive. (Unless you are with God's program it IS offensive.) God, being holy, couldn't tolerate their being near Him, so rather than the Covenant being a blessing it became a cursing. Coming to the conclusion it was nothing but death and destruction to them, they sent it back to Israel on a new cart pulled by two milk cows.

As the cart slowly approached Bethshemite the townspeople saw it while they harvested wheat in the valley. Excitedly they cried, "The Ark is coming," and they were glad to see it. (No one appreciates their weaknesses until they see what their fulness could have been.) The cart clattered on awkwardly to a field owned by a man named Joshua. Stopping by a large stone, the Levites, remembering it was their job to transport the Ark on staves between their shoulders, broke the cart up and offered the cows as a sacrifice. The first sacrifice and shedding of blood that was acceptable in more than twenty years.

They set the Ark on that large stone. Perched high on that rock they rejoiced and offered sacrifices to the Lord. What a picture! Joshua was the Hebrew name of Jesus, Jehovah's salvation. And with them we now "rejoice with a joyful noise unto the rock of our salvation" (Ps. 95:1), who is Jesus.

Just because the Ark of the Covenant was among them again, doesn't mean that this was the finality of what God had for them. That Ark was destined for a final place in Zion, in Jerusalem, many miles down the road.

It's too easy to accept what God is doing in part and call it the whole. Too easy for folk to be Spirit-filled and sing, "this is like heaven to me," when all they have are "mercy drops." There's a whole ocean waiting out there in the full purposes of God. Certainly the Israelites were happy and they had a right to be, but they didn't realize the Ark still had a long way to go.

I thank God for what He's doing today. The restoration

of His presence, rejoicing, faith living, power, glory and praise, but none of these things are the end in themselves. Prayer groups are unified with one another; churches are beginning to open and the talk of fellowship is wonderful, but there's more. Let's not make progress with two heel marks in the sand as God drags His dear children along. The Ark must set in David's Tabernacle on Mt. Zion, in the City of God.

Zion, of course, is wherever God's people are gathered together in divine order. Paul wrote in Hebrews 12:22-24: "But you have come to Mount Zion and to the city of the living God, the heavenly Jerusalem, and to myriads of angels, to the general assembly and church of the first-born who are enrolled in heaven, and to God, the judge of all, and to the spirit of righteous men made perfect, and to Jesus, the mediator of a new covenant, and to the sprinkled blood, which speaks better than the blood of Abel."

What a sentence!

But there it is! A restored Body, the modern-day Ark, which is Zion, the city, and Jesus the mediator of a better covenant. The Ark continues to be the place of His presence.

God has provided a special atmosphere in which He manifests Himself. It is praise!

Chapter Five

Heaven's Trademark

"Sing for joy in the Lord, O you righteous ones, praise is becoming to the upright. Give thanks to the Lord with the lyre; sing praises to Him with a harp of ten strings. Sing to Him a new song; play skillfully with a shout of joy. For the word of the Lord is upright; and all His work is done in faithfulness. He loves righteousness and justice; the earth is full of the loving-kindness of the Lord" (Ps. 33:1-5 NAS).

Some years ago when this ministry was new I learned how to take the spiritual temperature of the congregation. As an evangelist I was a specialist, called in when the sheep needed special attention. Vital signs are necessary for proper diagnosis so I learned how to recognize them. When I arrived for the first service I'd sit quietly on the platform, almost detached from the rest of the activities, "watching and praying," yet wholly conscious of the people.

I wasn't observing their conscious actions (they're usually controlled) but I was watching their unconscious reactions, always a true indicator of what is within. If there wasn't any evidence of a flowing biblical praise then I knew where I must begin.

God has purposed to do nothing for or through His people except through faith. "They that come to Him must believe that He is a rewarder of them that diligently seek Him"

(Heb. 11:6). One of the first principles I learned was that praise is the natural outflow of a faith-filled heart that was operating in the Word of God. Anyone believing the Word and acting on it, can't help it; they'll praise God! And the stronger the faith, the more reverberating the praise becomes.

So I prayed, "Lord, I need wisdom and a special anointing to both teach and lead these people into Your presence. They love You or they wouldn't be here, but it's obvious they aren't aware of You. Unless they learn how to enter into Your presence according to Your Word, the unsaved won't be convicted, much less converted."

Until the body comes together in the unity of real fellowship and worship nothing of much account happens. That genuine love, concern, fellowship and mutual worship is called the "garment of the saints" or the "symbol of the saints." It is their identifying trademark. Everywhere, in any age, praise has been the trademark, the testimony, the identifying mark of God's people. Where there is praise there is God, enthroned on those praises. In Psalm 81:5 we read, "This (praise) He ordained in Joseph for a testimony." Around the world magnificent cathedral windows are inscribed *TO THE GLORY OF GOD,* but the Bible declares that "we are the glory of God" (Eph. 1:12), never the building.

Contrary to many cherished beliefs, God has not chosen "power" as the trademark of His people. But both in heaven and on earth praise is the joint testimony according to Revelation 19:1-10. The Corinthian church illustrates this point. They were deeply involved in charismatic manifestations and power while still embroiled in sectarianism. Some said, "I follow Peter, what a preacher he is." Another said, "Nah, he's a piker. Paul's my boy. Have you ever seen a bolder man of God?" And yet others said, "You guys are dummies. Me? I'm spiritual. I just follow Jesus."

Had they been grounded in true praise they could have avoided all that. Nothing unifies like true worship. What else blends so many people with such diversified backgrounds together like praise? But we don't blame the Corinthians. You see, they were ignorant about these things. Paul told them he didn't want them to remain uninformed about such things (I Cor. 12:1).

It's out of the atmosphere of praise that the manifestation of true divine power freely flows meeting the needs of God's people. If we'll give Him first place, His authority automatically follows.

Let's take a look at this passage and see how these principles operate in the realm of praise-faith.

SING FOR JOY

The Psalmist doesn't say that after I have joy I'll sing, but I'll sing *for* joy. It's like the little boy in literature who had to sing for his supper. He didn't sing because he already had his supper but in order to get his supper. In like manner, the saints don't sing because they are necessarily happy, but in order to have joy expressed. If God depended on our singing because we already had joy, there wouldn't be much singing.

Natural people, that is, people governed by their senses, think they must be happy *before* they can sing or dance. But not the Psalmist. He often ordered himself to "sing for joy," or "dance for joy," or "soul, praise the Lord before I humble you with fasting and prayer." Strange isn't it? So diverse from one's normal reactions which move according to inner feelings.

Happiness, according to psychologists and behavior scientists, depends on external circumstances, "Everything's going my way so I'm happy today." Joy, however, isn't dependent on our situations but on the "Christ who dwells within!"

"But how can I sing for joy when I don't feel like I have any? Life's been hard on me. You just don't understand the troubles I've seen. Joy? Hah!"

Suppose "one of those days" was one when you had a little accident, about $350 worth, and immediately after the mishap you discover the insurance premium was in default. Somehow the premium notice was misplaced and unpaid. Oh, joy! No insurance! And there's the threat of a massive layoff at work and you've just purchased that long-wanted new home. With the closing costs practically emptying the savings account, who can "sing for joy?"

So you don't feel very enthused. No one said you had to—at this stage anyway. So your inner joy is so deep that even God has to search for it. *THAT'S THE TIME TO PRAISE THE LORD!* The Scripture says, "Praise is becoming for the upright." In other words, it's attractive, proper, comely; it works for you! Read verses 18 and 19: "Behold, the eye of the Lord is on those who fear Him, on those who hope for His lovingkindness; to deliver their soul from death, and to keep them alive in famine" (Ps. 33).

That's some promise. Guaranteed help in the time of trouble, and deliverance from *any* problem. But notice, however, it's directly related to obeying the principles found in verses 1-5, our text, which begins with, *Sing for joy!*

Did you know the "joy of the Lord is our strength?" (Neh. 8:10). That's why Jesus was so concerned about His disciples having that joy. Without it the saints are weak but with it they are "little lions." So they were made to understand what He was doing for them. "My joy I give to you that your joy may be full." Was this joy based on their external circumstances? Hardly! They were in it together, and the gospels reveal that the Lord's ministry on earth was finished in three years. Happy circumstances? Rather it was one of constant conflict. Their joy was to be *in* the victorious Christ. And that joy is also yours for the asking. He promised, "My joy I give them" (John 17:13).

Everything is received by faith whether salvation,

deliverance, prosperity, or the promise of the Holy Spirit. All are appropriated by faith. And that "word of faith" is "confessing with the mouth and believing with the heart" (Rom. 10:10). It's simply an unchangeable law of the Spirit that faith operates through your mouth. You speak first, according to the Word, resulting in believing with the heart. I've found no better way to overcome my mental doubts than to fill my spirit with the Word until my inner man is abundantly filled. Then out of that abundance my mouth speaks, either as a command of authority, or praise. Paul calls this "the word of faith." But notice what happens.

Since it's impossible to think one thing and say another, whatever you say is what you'll begin thinking. Please don't ask me to explain HOW that works, it just does. When your thoughts are drifting, when unbelief rears its ugly head, when doubt questions the integrity of the Word, verbally begin to confess the Word. It won't be long before a miracle takes place in your thinking. Your thoughts will change. As one brother said, "We have a miracle in our mouth."

Even as the "law of faith" operates through man's mouth, joy also comes the same way. The difference is this: whereas we mentioned men talk doubt in the previous paragraph, we're now speaking of feelings. That spoken, expressed joy in your inner man, becomes praise unto the Lord, and releases His power and promise into the situation.

Believe in your heart that the promise of Psalm 33:18, 19 is yours and then SING FOR JOY about it! As though you already had it! This, I believe, is the reason so many believers are weak. They have no joy, consequently they have no strength. Paul said he wanted to finish his course with joy (Acts 20:23, 24) but all he had were trials, battles and hardships in his life.

Joy must be perfected, or matured, according to John 17:13. When completed it will be as steadfast as Jesus' was. Our joy is matured exactly as His was. Through usage in battle. That SINGING FOR JOY is an act of your will, the deliberate practice of your mouth, regardless of your head faith.

But how? SING FOR JOY IN THE LORD.

No one is expected to "rejoice always" in their own strength. It's impossible to have joy in the midst of life's circumstances in your own power. It must be *in the Lord.*

You accept what Jesus has done *for* you; rest in it; trust in it; thank Him for it, and you'll soon have the joy of it! No part of this can be avoided. What Jesus has done for us is declared in the Word. That's the beginning source, the Word. Because He's already cried, "It is finished," I can rest in it. So I'll thank Him for it. By confessing my grateful attitude for the Word and Him, I'll just trust Him. And miracle of miracles, there's the joy.

It has nothing to do with the outward circumstances. They may, or may not change immediately; they will eventually. That's His promise. Happiness depends on those external situations while joy is an inward quality, a fruit of the Spirit, a product of the Christ within you, the hope of glory!

Happiness is based on freedom from stress, absence of problems, avoiding unfavorable circumstances and conflicts, while JOY is the confidence we have that "greater is He who is in me than he who is in the world." Therefore, joy doesn't look on outward problems, but inward possibilities.

It's obedience to this principle that lifts your heavy, mourning soul because you've been anointed with the "oil of gladness, the mantle of praise, instead of the spirit of heaviness" (Isa. 61:1-3). There *will* be inner JOY because obedient praise always lifts the broken spirit heavenward.

Paul and Silas sat, not because they wanted to, in the inner prison in Philippi, beaten from their heads to their heels. Their hands and feet were uncomfortably locked together in stocks. Midnight has come, eerie dark, dank with the smell of unclean bodies housed in a room far too small. It was close and utterly filthy.

"Hey, Paul," Silas asked loudly, "Got your pitch pipe?"

"You kidding? It's in my left pocket but how do you propose I can get it? Why?"

"Well, it's midnight or thereabouts. Just got to thinking. That's the time David used to get up and praise the Lord. And I've been thinking, Paul. Do you realize how good God has been to us? Completely setting us free from those powers of darkness, and actually enrolling us in the Kingdom of God? Let's just praise the Lord!"

"I'm for that," Paul responded, momentarily forgetting the excruciating pain in his back. Some 39 stripes had been laid there with the execution whip hours earlier for preaching about Jesus. So lifting their voices they *sang for joy in the Lord.*

Were they happy? Did they have a right to feel rejected? In the natural, yes, but you see they weren't natural men. When believers are supernaturally anointed then they become more natural than they naturally are. Were they joyful? Absolutely! Simply because they recognized their strength wasn't in themselves but in the Christ who was *in* them. They knew where He was, and were assured that He was the Lord of the circumstance.

They sang for joy and the prisoners heard them. But more than that, God heard them! Now He who inhabits the praises of His people, He who puts all things together, took some of it apart. In case you're not familiar with the ending, the Lord entered that prison in liberating power. A strange earthquake shook the place, destroying it, yet no one was hurt. Doors flew open, bonds slipped off the men, and the prisoners, all of them, were mysteriously set free.

The Word is filled with examples of men who maintained the trademark of the saints, regardless of the hopelessness of their situation.

Peter was another jailbreaker who pulled a spiritual

"Houdini" while the local church prayed and praised. They weren't rejoicing *because* he was in jail, but because the Lord of the prison would *deliver* him! Their vision wasn't horizontal, facing and observing the problem, but vertical, seeing Him high and lifted up as Lord over all!

Years later Rome tried to claim Paul as their prisoner. I can almost hear that determined man declaring: "Sorry, Caesar, you'll have to wait for another time. I'm already the prisoner of Jesus Christ. I can't possibly accommodate you."

"Are you crazy, man? Don't you realize my chains are on you? How can you say you're not my prisoner?" Rome replied indignantly.

"Simple, sir, you have my physical man, but Jesus has the real me. You can control my circumstances but no one, I mean no one, can touch my inner man. Excuse me while I take time out and rejoice and praise God. Oops—sorry about that—forgot about those chains. Well, I can't do much dancing on the outside but I'll sure do some on the inside. Glory!"

Jehoshaphat praised God in the face of immediate defeat. Surrounded by three armies he stopped and praised the Lord. Instead of the soldiers using their arms to pull their bows and cock their arrows, they raised their hands and praised the Lord with a loud voice. (I sometimes wonder whether the enemy wasn't routed and turned on one another in argument because of such a "dumb" way to fight.) Jehoshaphat's praise became a self-rewarding act of faith.

While Israel shouted the praise of God, the walls of Jericho fell flat. They literally shouted the wall down rather than wait for the wall to fall down flat and then shout.

Joseph praised God while *in* Egypt's prison, and was elevated to prime minister.

John praised God from his exile and supposed death on Patmos. Instead of whimpering about his fate he was filled with the Spirit and ended up receiving the Book of Revelation.

Job praised God while his body was covered with boils, and not only received a healing but restored prosperity.

The three Hebrew children praised God with a hot dance in the midst of the furnace.

Daniel decided to praise God while the lions waited to dine on him.

Most saints, rather than bearing the trademark of joy in the Lord, reflect defeat, discouragement and outright failure. If we'd but realize that in Christ Jesus we'll never be more righteous than we are right now, we'd cease putting ourselves down. No one ever grows into righteousness. You can grow into maturity but never into righteousness. That's because the Word declares you already are righteous! "But now apart from the law the righteousness of God has been manifested . . . even the righteousness of God through faith in Jesus Christ for all those who believe" (Rom. 3:21, 22 NAS).

Righteousness is the ability to stand in His presence without any attitude of inferiority, unworthiness, incompleteness or failure. It is the life of Christ in you (Col. 1:27). And in Psalm 33:1 it is the Lord Himself, who says you are righteous. So stop condemning yourself. Stop blaming yourself for your failures.

When you comprehend the fact that God *is* careful to perform His promises; that His Word declares you righteous, then you can sing for joy and that *joy* becomes your *trademark!* It is becoming to the upright.

PRAISE IS COMELY TO THE UPRIGHT

Comely, according to the dictionary, means proper attire, attractiveness, appearance. Praise then, is how one recognizes the upright.

Recently, I read an interesting psychological report that said if you want to know what other people are really thinking, mimic their facial expressions. You'll soon begin to feel as they feel. I don't know how accurate this is but it caught my eye. This, I suppose, is the role of character acting and perhaps is the reason so many actors are emotionally unstable with ever changing tastes and families. Their frequent play-acting of fictitious characters works on their subconscious and it isn't long before they become the part they're playing. The article went on to say that everyone has certain attitudes, and their facial expressions generally reflect what is in them, what they're thinking. This has given rise to the science (?) of body language.

This agrees with the Word. "Out of the abundance of the heart the mouth speaks," and what man speaks he will soon become. You are today what you've been thinking and saying in the past. No more and no less, but exactly what you've been confessing. If this principle works negatively, it follows that it must work positively, also. If I, by mimicking someone's facial expression can experience their feelings, what would happen if I, by an act of my will in line with the Word of God, bring my outer man into harmony with it? Judson Cornwall once shared a little story that illustrates this.

Seems that on a certain blue Monday a dad arose before his wife, prepared his own breakfast, and went to work. This wasn't a common practice, only that his wife needed the extra rest. He cracked an egg and missed—splat— it hit the floor, gooky mess, since the kitchen was covered with carpet. *Bounty* did its best—it's stronger you know—but it left a tell-tale yellow mess for his uncomplaining wife to finish. He finished his breakfast and didn't do too badly, except for the strawberry jam in the middle of Ann Landers, which cemented the rest of the paper together.

When his wife finally got up, she was late because he forgot to call her. So her exciting day began a half hour late. She managed to get the kids off to school, but that mess . . .

Finally, off to work herself. On the way, however, she had a flat. See that this was a special blue, bluer, bluest Monday? And this not being the era of gallant masculinity, no one stopped and offered to change the tire for her. (If any of you have ever changed a tire you know what it can do to clean clothes.) When she finally arrived at her job she walked with a too-determined step, her lips pursed into a fine line—were there any lips at all?—and she was 45 minutes late. Her hair? Well, some strands were floating as she walked, maybe quite a few, really, and her hands were more than dusty, but worst of all, know who was waiting for her? The boss—glaring. Happy? Are you kidding? Joy? Where and for that matter, why?

But, after some fifteen or more minutes in the repair shop (that's the powder room), she put on a new complexion, set her hair back in place, sprinkled a dab of fresh Avon behind her ears, and faced the world. How? Well, you see, her job was the welcoming person at the complaint desk in a department store. She didn't feel like smiling but that's what she was paid to do, so almost with an act of defiance she pulled her cheeks apart with her fingers, forced a sort of plastic smile and greeted her first customer.

"Good morning, sir. Lovely morning, isn't it? O, it isn't? May I help you? You've received *this* piece of shoddy merchandise? We're so sorry. Here, you sit right here. Have a cup of coffee? Cream? No? I'll be right back with another perfect item for you." Before he could say, "Oh, joy," she was smilingly walking away.

Don't you know that his incoming scowl became an outgoing smile? Listen: he's even talking to himself. "Not a bad store after all. Said I wouldn't come here again, but I believe I will. Nice folk here!"

Her purpose, you see, was to make upset folks settle down. That defective product could cost them more than one customer; maybe they have an army of relatives. But her smiling, pleasant, understanding face has a way of disarming you.

Now ask me how come I know it works that way?

More than that, something happened to her. It wasn't but just a few minutes after she put that smile on her face, she felt good herself. The problems were still there, but her countenance changed and she looked differently. That smile she deliberately put on her face somehow changed her whole outlook.

Now you know why the Scripture says, "The joy of the Lord is our strength!"

You and I are the expression of the joy and victory of Jesus Christ. Who in the world is going to want what we have if we walk around looking religious, poker-faced, expressionless, almost as though God was old, nervous, and hard to get along with?

The story is told of a Christian person doing street work in New York City when she spotted a fellow who was too full of the wrong spirits. She headed for him, determined and concerned. Her street ministry was no game but serious business. She talked to him some ten minutes, holding his attention by not releasing the tract she gave him.

"Sir, wouldn't you like to accept Jesus as your Lord and let Him rescue you?" she queried almost pathetically.

Studying her face through blurred eyes he said, "Sorry, lady, I've got enough troubles now without getting what *you've* got."

When I first heard that I said, "Yeah!" but in the following years I've met too many just like that. No joy! All work! Sinners are defaulting Christianity after looking at the saints who sing for sorrow! "Here I wander far below, midst my troubles, cares and woes, but at the end of the road, there's God!" Now isn't that exciting? Thank God it's changing. There are Bob Harringtons telling the world: *It's fun being saved.*

So you see praise is the symbol, the outward appearance of the saints and *God likes it that way!*

Chapter Six

Praise Is Faith at Work

We are told in Scripture, "He who offers a sacrifice of thanksgiving honors Me; and to him who orders his way a-right, I shall show the salvation of God" (Ps. 50:23 NAS). "Let the people praise thee, O God; let all the people praise thee. Then shall the earth yield her increase; and God, even our own God, shall bless us" (Ps. 67:5, 6 KJV).

Everywhere I minister I meet dear Christians who are trying to believe the Lord. Their needs are great, ranging from unsaved families to sickness and poverty. They accept the Bible promises, intellectually, at least. Many have prayed for years; some have even fasted to the point of discouragement, yet the answer doesn't come.

"What's the problem, Chuck? I'm doing everything I know to do. Is there some hidden sin in my life that's keeping God from answering my prayers? I've prayed again and again and again. What's wrong?" I am frequently asked.

It doesn't take long to uncover the problem, and no, I'm not oversimplifying the problem.

There are two extremes that entrap most believers. One is presumptuousness, and the other is negativeness. The first runs the gauntlet from taking God for granted and demanding that He must obey you—after all I have my covenant rights—to the person so plagued by unbelief and tradition that they wonder about their wonder. In between there's the spurious counterfeit offering penance for sins they plan on committing again, to the Bible thumper who believes every jot and tittle with a clenched fist and angry heart who is ready to "contend for the faith." And also there's the practicing "clothesline religionist" whose heart is filled with a "perfect love" that is so bitter it poisons everything it touches. Faith does work by love but not that kind. And finally, there's the pseudo-intellectual who thinks he knows more about what Jesus meant than Jesus did Himself.

The problem of negativeness, a definite form of doubt and unbelief, springs from words and actions that belittle both the person's testimony and the Word of God they profess to believe. Both presumption and negativeness destroy faith and praise, but praise, acting as a release for true faith will cure both.

Praise is more than a casual point of contact, more than a cure-all, more than a formula for manipulating the Word of God, but a life style, the life of living faith.

What we're dealing with is a step beyond resting in God's goodness. It's acceptance of His will for us to be sure, but launches into the active application of His Word. God is against evil, sin, sickness, death, broken homes, poverty, disease and heartache. He is against the "curse," having delivered us from the curse (Gal. 3:13). Our application of praise as faith at work will cause the Word to come alive. You'll be saying, "I praise you, Lord, because you've already blessed me, and I thank you that I'm entering into that blessing now!" (Eph. 1:3).

In our text there are at least five obvious principles and promises:

1. Our will is involved, "he who offers."

2. A sacrifice is offered which costs us something dear.

3. Honors, glorifies God. It exalts Him, leans on His Word, recognizes Him as the source, glorifies Him and releases

Him into your situation by lifting you out of yours into His.

4. Then, our actions and our conversation must agree with our offering.

5. The answer is guaranteed and forthcoming.

Sound familiar? It's another one of those amazing proofs that the Bible is divinely inspired. The Psalmist expresses the same principle that Jesus, years later, uttered in Mark 11:24. "Therefore, I say to you, all things for which you pray and ask, believe that you have received them, and they shall be granted you" (NAS).

- You ask because your will is involved.
- You offer to Him something, you trust in His Word through praise.
- It honors God when you believe you've received the promises before you have them.
- You believe, trust, strongly rely on, and adhere to steadfastly.
- They shall be granted you.

GOD'S PROMISES ARE FOR THE OBEDIENT

In Psalm 50 there's a contrast between the obedient and the rebellious. "What right have you to tell of My statutes, and to take My covenant in your mouth?" (v. 16) the Lord asks the wicked. (At least they weren't ignorant of the covenant promises. They knew it was a legal contract between God and man with both sides of the commitment spelled out. They knew that the covenant must be confessed, ("in your mouth") "For you hate discipline, and you cast My words behind you. When you see a thief, you are pleased with him, and you associate with adulterers. You let your mouth loose in evil, and your tongue frames deceit. You sit and speak against your brother; you slander your own mother's son. These things you have done, and I kept silence; you thought I was just like you" (vv. 17-21 NAS).

Why weren't the irrevocable covenant promises working?

72

Their mouths were filled with negative talk, gossip, criticism, and hatefulness. And what caused such a state? They hated discipline and refused to submit their wills to the Word of God, therefore, they cast the Word behind them.

Had they walked in praise and thanksgiving this could not have happened. It's impossible to gossip when your mouth is filled with praise. How can one deny the Word of God when they're using it as praise unto Him? "Faith cometh by hearing and hearing by the Word of God" (Rom. 10:14). Is it possible to fellowship with the Christ rejecters when your lips are continually filled with praise? They won't stay around and listen.

It finally got so bad when God mercifully withheld His judgments that Israel equated God with them. "You thought I was just like you," He charged them in Ps. 50:21. How many people have also gone so long without praising God that they assume He doesn't like it either?

You see, God never moves out of turn, but He always moves when it is His turn. Our faith expects Him to do His part when we obey. But again, man tends to run to extremes. We either think our part is some physical effort to please God as a form of righteousness, or we sit back and do nothing, in substance blaming everything that comes into our lives, either good or bad, as allowed by Him, therefore of Him.

If a man's body is filled with cancer, his children on drugs, and his wife unfaithful, would that be God's will for him and should he submit to it? No way! Not when such a tremendous price has been paid for our deliverance from these works of darkness. "We have been delivered from the authority of darkness (the kingdom and works of Satan) and delivered into the Kingdom of His Son" (the kingdom of God) (Col. 1:13). This is past tense, and readily available to all who believe.

We should never thank God for the evil which Satan

does or inspires. But in that plight we are provided the opportunity to stand secure in God's Word, looking forward to His deliverance, while we thank Him ahead of time, thereby honoring Him. This is Bible faith in action!

I'll be the first to declare that no one can twist God's arm behind His back with praise. Neither is it suggested that it's a cure-all like some antique patent medicine, but to insist that we never praise or thank God for expected results and promises is to flout the entire New Testament teaching on the law of faith. To passively sit back and accept whatever happens in your life as His loving, perfect will reduces the soldier "fighting the good fight of faith" to that of a zombie, much like a nursery infant totally dominated by his attendants. Rather, God has purposed that we grow toward maturity whereby we don't continually cry for deliverance from our problems, but in them become the master of them, thereby exercising the authority, dominion and power Jesus willed us.

James said, "resist the devil and he will flee from you" (James 4:7). "This is the victory that overcometh the world, even our faith" (I John 5:4). Revelation 12:11 says, "They overcame him (the devil) by the blood of the Lamb and by the word of their testimony." Faith in the blood of Jesus, faith in the Word, and faith in the power of the Spirit will cause the devil to flee every time. I Peter 5:9 says we are to steadfastly resist the devil. Not once does the Bible suggest we sit back and give in, but wage war because God says the devil will flee if we resist him. And praise is proven to be one of the most potent weapons available to the saints.

It's to those who "delight themselves in the Lord that He gives the desires of the heart" (Ps. 37:4); to those who "diligently hearken to the voice (WORD) of the Lord," and "do that which is right in His sight" that "the Lord will take away from thee all sicknesses," and the curse (see Deuteronomy 7:15; Exodus 15:26; Galatians 3:8).

Praise then, is an expression of faith that flows from an obedient heart! Just as it's impossible to praise the Lord and frown, so it's impossible to regard rebellion in your heart and thank the Lord. Paul said that by obeying "it may be well with thee, and thou mayest live long on the earth" (Eph. 6:3). To those who "walk uprightly," it is said, "no good thing will He withhold" (Ps. 84:11).

If faith is the cohesive fusion of the heart and will with God's will as declared in His Word, then where this union is absent, results are impossible. This is a spiritual law and it's just as everlasting as any covenant God ever made with man. My spirit and my will must submit to His Word! That is faith! Therefore, "He keepeth covenant and mercy with them that love Him and keep his commandments to a thousand generations" (Deut. 7:9). So if my heart is perfect toward Him then the eyes of the Lord run to and fro throughout the whole earth to show Himself strong on my behalf (2 Chron. 16:9).

Some years ago S. D. Gordon wrote a little booklet, *Prayer Changes Things,* and to be sure, it does. That phrase has become a motto in many homes. No one disputes the fact that prayer, true believing prayer, does change persons, moves mountains and things. But we are likewise aware, that many times, prayer alone hasn't moved the enemy one inch from his stronghold.

It was during a horrible ordeal that I learned, by trial and error, this wonderful truth: *praise finishes what prayer begins!* If you've read *Kicked Out Of The Kingdom* you'll recall the chapter narrating my son's motorcycle accident. One Saturday night, coming home from work, he plowed his bike into the side of a drunk driver's car, going through the windshield from the outside in.

When we first saw him at the emergency room at Sarasota Memorial, at least two surgeons had bypassed him as "too far gone." He was literally drowning in his own blood, and had an unbelievable amount of skull and brain damage.

A hastily-called neurosurgeon informed us that there wasn't much we could expect. After viewing the x-rays he pointed out the massive fractures and a clot near the center of the brain. He later told us that the right menningal artery was severed and the brain was mushy. His words were, "The boy's brain is shredded. I've repaired it the best I know how."

After completing a craniotomy in less than half the normal time he met us in the chapel and told us the worst.

"Reverend, if he lives he won't remember a thing before the accident. I suspect a permanent loss of memory, but I'm more concerned about his body function. He has such massive brain damage that the left side of his body . . . I doubt if he'll use it again. I'm sorry so don't even expect or hope."

Hourly we visited him in the intensive care unit. Others were there with their loved ones, also. Everyone of them looking as though the end of their world was at hand, and for many of them it was.

David drifted into a deep coma, his body deathly still. Prayer had gone up steadily from both our hearts and mouths, and we were coming to the place where it was difficult to pray any more. My desire was for the Word of God to prevail. I didn't have the slightest doubt that the Word was true, but whenever I looked at that broken body with its grotesquely swollen head, the deep, sunken eyes, the dried blood embedded around the braces on his teeth, and the gurgling sound of the oxygen being forced into his lungs through a hole in his throat, my senses reeled. Did I doubt? I don't think so, but it was difficult to tell. I was numb!

Not once did I question God as to why this happened. There was no whimpering, nor did I torment myself with unanswerable questions. But in this plight I saw an opportunity for the Lord of the Word to prevail. And then I began to discover there's another side.

My prayer wing was pretty well developed, but I was

still bound. Truth is, I was flopping around in a circle like a bird with a broken wing. Neither my wife nor I fainted during those endless hours, our prayers sustained us, but we needed something more.

It was then I read a statement by E. W. Kenyon that said, *PRAYER ASKS BUT PRAISE TAKES. PRAYER TALKS ABOUT THE PROBLEM BUT PRAISE TAKES THE ANSWER FROM GOD.* I learned that the time to praise God was when the pressure is the greatest, when the valley is the darkest, so praise Him we did. For what?

I didn't praise God for my son's accident, couldn't find Scripture to warrant that. Neither did we praise God for his broken body. That was the work of Satan who comes only to steal, destroy and kill. But I did thank God that He would prevail, His Word vindicated and the "impossible become possible to them that believe."

From that moment we didn't consciously ask God for His healing and restoration again. It was thanksgiving that His Word declared it already done. It was *FAITH IN ACTION THROUGH PRAISE.*

Consequently we were lifted from the negative circumstances of our wrecked world into the glorious life of His world. Our senses were directed toward God. Our vision was upward rather than downward. We were seated with Him in heavenly places, watching the salvation of the Lord manifested.

When Peter prayed for Dorcas who had died, he sent everyone from the room. Then he turned away from the body and prayed for her deliverance. After he completed his prayer, and knew the authority was there to raise her, he then turned to the body and ordered her to get up. And she did! Had he stared at the corpse while he prayed I'm certain his senses would have played tricks on him. Instead, he turned away, looked toward the Father and thanked Him for hearing him.

Had Peter passively accepted her death as the perfect

will of God for the moment; had he audibly confessed and thanked God that she was dead, unless God arbitrarily raised her, she would have remained dead. Peter would never have exercised authority and faith over her dead body. He would have accepted it as the plan of God and just let God work it out His own way. That is okay, and it will work, but it isn't the walk of faith, nor is it fully pleasing to God according to Hebrews 11:6. We must believe, act on that belief that He will reward those who seek Him. Scripture says, "He watches over His Word and is careful to perform it" (Jer. 1:12).

I learned that praise is the most efficient follow-up to my requests. We refused to consider my son's body, much less the admonition of the nursing staff. "He can't make it; he won't make it. If he does make it he won't be normal."

We lifted our faces toward God and said, "Father, You've never failed us yet, and You never will. We have a covenant with You and we're completely dependent on You. We don't understand all this yet, but this we know, we trust You and confess You as Lord of this conflict. You're the healer, the deliverer, the restorer, the God of the perfect and the living. Therefore, bring him forth, completely whole!" And we began praising the Lord that He would!

Whenever doubt reared its ugly head we praised all the stronger. When time passed without any visible change we continually praised. "I will bless the Lord at all times: his praise shall continually be in my mouth . . . . I sought the Lord, and he heard me, and delivered me from all my fears" (Ps. 34:1, 4). My fears that we weren't doing something right; my fears that perhaps God wouldn't because David had done something extra wrong. All my fears. All my condemnation. All my thoughts during the long, lonely nights. We continued our praise.

The results? Total, perfect healing on the seventeenth day, but oh, the battle! What a sacrifice!

THE SACRIFICE OF PRAISE

Whenever something costs you dearly, that's a sacrifice, and the Lord is teaching us to offer to Him the *SACRIFICE OF PRAISE*. The Bible commands us, "By him therefore let us offer the sacrifice of praise to God continually, that is, the fruit of our lips giving thanks to his name" (Heb. 13:15).

Too often prayer without praise becomes the whine of fear, the groan of the beggar, but prayer with praise is offering to God our best. Ending prayer with praise is sealing what you've asked in faith with a period while you wait, expectantly for delivery. After you've asked in prayer and the answer still seems a zillion miles away, when the clouds seem so dark and thick that no amount of sunshine pierces them; when heaven is as cold and hard as ice, that is the time to offer Him the *SACRIFICE OF PRAISE*.

No, it is not taking the bull by the horns and trying to force God to do what you want. Real prayer is simply agreeing with the Word which already expressed His will. When you pray according to the Word it's absolutely impossible to miss His will.

The reason then, when in the light of a completed redemption, that we still have these uphill fights, is because we've listened to the wrong voice. Rather than listen to the "father of lies," why not make him listen to you as you glorify the "Father of life!"

When Satan tempted our Lord Jesus He used the Word against him. Satan used it negatively by casting a shadow of doubt around it. "Did God say?" has always been his favorite attack. Generally though, instead of confronting you personally as he did Jesus in the wilderness, he uses some fellow believer.

What did he say to Jesus? "IF, IF, IF you're the Son of God, why don't you do this? IF, IF, IF: . . ." With Eve, where he began his trickery he suggested, "Did God really say that? I wonder if that is what He really meant?" Notice his psychology! He doesn't try to get you to deny the Word completely, but only entertain a slight doubt about it. "Can God be trusted? Is His Word really good? *IF, IF, IF, IF, WHAT IF?*"

I remember an elderly lady in the first church I pastored who had this problem. She came into the Spirit walk under this ministry, and oh, how she loved Jesus! She was 70 before she discovered Jesus was really a friendly Person who was interested in her. Being an old maid, she really appreciated her times of fellowship with Him. But one morning right after church, she pulled on my sleeve.

"Pastor, He doesn't love me any more!" Her eyes were flashing, as she attempted to stifle her inner hurt.

"What do you mean, He doesn't love you any more? Who? Jesus? That's impossible!"

"Now don't you dare tell me it's impossible. I'm involved," she pouted. "He hasn't spoken to me for three days." Then she broke into tears. "What have I done wrong? What *IF* He never speaks to me again? Why doesn't He talk to me?"

Somehow I discerned her problem was an example of what we're talking about so I told her to just hold steady and I'd come over and talk with her, just as soon as church was over and I got a bite of lunch.

Later that afternoon I almost shuddered at the prospect. Although this dear lady loved Jesus with a love very few comprehended, she had a "snappy" side to her nature and I didn't have the grace to deal with that.

"What makes you think He hasn't been listening to you?" I questioned her.

"Well, He hasn't spoken to me for three days. I'm worried. I don't believe I could live without Him talking to me."

After reasoning with her it became evident that Satan had lied to her, and she fell for the trick. The moment you open up to his deceptions it's difficult to shake them. Something drastic had to be done.

"Well, now," I suggested. "If He isn't listening to you, then it doesn't really make any difference what you say to Him, does it?" She glared at me curiously. "So why don't you lift your face toward Him and just start cursing?!"

"Now, Pastor," she snapped immediately, "you know I can't do that!"

I knew she couldn't even for natural reasons. It wasn't her style, even as an unbeliever, to curse, so I forced the issue, expecting a violent reaction.

"Don't be afraid! He can't hear you, or, at least you said He wouldn't hear *you*!" I stepped back and observed her reaction.

Slowly the lie vanished, *IF, IF, IF, WHAT IF, WHAT IF, HE WON'T, HE WON'T. HE DOESN'T LOVE YOU ANY MORE.* In its place came the realization that He had heard her. If He didn't then even her cursing would escape His understanding. Slowly a grin crossed her face. "You tricked me! But I see it now! He does hear me. It was because I took my eyes from Him and I listened to my doubts."

Then together we offered to God the *SACRIFICE OF PRAISE,* thanking Him.

Satan knew who Jesus was without questioning the *IF* you are the Son of God, and he knew this dear lady WAS God's child, but he knew that if he could get either of them to doubt for a moment, they would be helpless before him. All he heard from Jesus' lips was, "It is written, it is written, it is written!" (Matt. 4:4, 7, 10). That ought to tell you something. The Word is the best defense we have.

"Then the devil left him, and behold, angels came and ministered unto him." And an example was left for us. Resist the devil, leave doubt and discouragement with the Word, and not only will Satan flee but ministering spirits will come and minister unto you.

Our problem is, rather than saying, "It is written," we

are prone to say, "The devil said," or "The devil did!" I tell you a truth, Christ's way is the only successful way to overcome! IT IS WRITTEN! In other words, *according to Thy Word, O Lord, I do believe. It's Your covenant, and I stand firmly upon it knowing you've pledged your sworn oath to make it good.*

If Jesus, as the pattern Son, told us that we should follow closely in his footsteps, and He overcame this way, can we do better? *SO LET THE DEVIL HEAR YOU OFFER THE SACRIFICE OF THANKSGIVING FOR VICTORY OVER HIM!* He won't stay around long and listen to the likes of that! We have two choices: we can refuse to offer the sacrifice of thanksgiving to the Lion of the tribe of Judah (which means praise), or accept the fear that comes from being chased by the roaring lion, walking about, seeking whom he may devour (I Peter 5:8).

HONORING GOD

How does this sacrifice of thanksgiving honor God, and how do my corresponding actions bring the answer?

Psalm 50:16 mentions the covenant being in our mouth. That is confession.

It honors God to believe Him even when our senses contradict Him. Yet He promises to deliver those who honor Him. In no way does this imply that we use praise as an arm-twister whereby we force God to act our way. This is presumptuousness and not faith. God promises to respond to faith/praise that trusts in His Word. Feelings can be absent yet He remains faithful. The progression has always been fact, faith, feeling—in that order. The fact is the Word, then faith in that word-fact, and the feeling will follow.

He sent His word and healed them (Psalm 107:20). He didn't give them feelings that they were healed. Abraham is called the father of the faithful because he maintained a steadfast confidence in the Word even though he had to wait twenty-five years for the promise to be fulfilled.

The praise that takes believes God has already given us all things pertaining to life and godliness. This includes everything we need for spirit, soul and body, and it honors the Father greatly to show forth this gratitude by praise.

In Mark 11:24 Jesus expresses the conditions required for the appropriation of any blessing. "What things soever you desire, when you pray, believe that you receive them, and you shall have them." Note the tenses: WHEN you pray (the fact) that is the now. Then believe you receive them, that you already have received them by the eye of *faith* and you *SHALL* have them, future (feeling).

Now this is the same pattern Psalm 50:23 follows. First, you ask by thanking and honoring God from the promise (fact). Then you expect to receive by acting accordingly with both vocal and physical manifestations (faith), and you shall receive them (feeling).

So the sacrifice of praise is thanking Him for what He said He would do so "you shall have them," Jesus said. This is your proof that you've not only been heard but that the answer is forthcoming.

To the faith man the Word of God *is* the voice of God. When the Word says *I will*, then that is the voice of God. We know we have the petition we desire of Him, not because we already have the answer, but because God is faithful who also will do it!

In Psalm 106:12 we read, "Then they believed his words; they sang his praise."

If we're going to praise God for a thing, we're going to have to walk in accordance or agreement with our praise-confession!

We can't be like the young fellow who got married, and right after the ceremony took the pastor aside and said, "I don't feel married."

"Well, friend," the kindly pastor replied, "I'll clue you,

83

you're married whether you feel like it or not, so you'd better accept your responsibilities." He had to order his ways aright. Getting up early in the morning and going to work when it would have been nice to lay in bed. Caring for another life as his own.

Our praise honors God because "it sees Him that is invisible." It's occupied with His power and mercy, never with human frailties. He invites you to take hold of His strength. "Let the weak say I am strong," even if they aren't! It's when we are weak that we ought to stand on the authority of the Word, and offer the sacrifice of praise saying, "I am strong, and His strength is made perfect in weaknesses."

ORDERING OUR WAYS ARIGHT

All praise, as an expression of faith, *MUST FIND A CORRESPONDING ACTION* in our daily walk. Frequently, when I face a new congregation I'll ask them, "How many of you have the joy of the Lord in your heart?" They'll usually respond by the raised hand. "Then how about notifying your face?" Instantly, they put corresponding actions to their joy and break into laughter, breaking the tension. If we're happy on the inside, we ought to look happy on the outside.

Scripture is filled with admonitions that we should act what we believe. "Rise, take up your bed and walk," Jesus commanded the sick man. "If ye then be raised with Christ, walk in newness of life," Paul admonished. Faith, praise, all spiritual forces must be expressed by our manner of life.

A young doctor came to me some time back. His practice was just beginning and had a need for further equipment, staff and office space. His current income was around $35,000 a year, which isn't much when all expenses are deducted.

"Chuck," said the doctor, "I'm believing God for a large increase in my yearly income. I'm believing for at least $50,000. Now as an act of my faith should I continue tithing on what I'm currently making, or on what I believe I will make?"

I paused for a moment before answering. No one had asked a question exactly like that before, but the principles are always the same. If you believe you will receive, then the eye of faith already possesses.

"Don, I believe you should begin tithing on what you believe you will receive inasmuch as you already have it according to the law of prayer and praise." So he immediately increased his giving accordingly, and it wasn't long before he was again increasing that tithe. Today, four years later, his income exceeds that amount many times.

In the King James Version Psalm 50:23 reads, "to him that ordereth his conversation aright," while it's translated as "ways" in modern translations. The latter is a better rendering, but both are correct. Conversation, when the KJV was published meant "your manner of living," the life-style. So what the Psalmist is saying is this. After you've offered the sacrifice of thanksgiving, then change your life-style to agree with your praise-confession. Put some legs to what you're saying.

Praise, actually, is a life-style. If there is faith in your heart and you fail to praise, sooner or later that faith will ebb until finally there's nothing left. On the other hand, there isn't anything I know that will increase your faith like Biblical praise. *Offering back to God His own Word as praise.* You must praise or you'll never know faith. Faith precedes praise and praise brings in the victory.

Romans 10:17 says that "faith comes from hearing and hearing by the word of God." *Word* here in the Greek is "rhema," or the spoken word. When you use the word as thanksgiving and praise, it focuses your attention away from circumstances and impossibilities to the Mighty God. If the saints would stop fretting and start letting God have His way, their lives would be revolutionized.

The secret then, if there is any, in the power of praise is

this: *ALL THE BLESSINGS OF GOD SPRING FROM THE LIFE OF GOD.*

Eternal life is "Christ in you the hope of glory."

Healing is His health and life in us.

Our joy is His joy; our peace is His peace; our prosperity is His riches; our righteousness is His. To be *in* Christ is to be *in* Life. Therefore, your praise WILL honor God and bring you into His Presence. By praising you'll conquer unbeliefs and doubts, resulting in a change in your thinking and conversation by agreeing with God rather than the circumstances. Consequently, God promises to show forth His salvation unto you! That is *FAITH IN ACTION THROUGH THE MEDIUM OF PRAISE.*

Chapter Seven

From Fear to Faith

What you read in this chapter may stun or shock you; it may amaze and surprise you, but one thing it will do, it will change your life. I trust you'll grasp the principles and practice them.

Please turn to 2 Chronicles 20:1-30 (NAS) and read the whole section. It's too long to quote here but you'll miss the value of this lesson if you don't read it.

Note especially verse 3: "And Jehoshaphat was *afraid* and turned his attention to seek the Lord; and proclaimed a fast throughout all Judah." Then in verse 30: "So the kingdom of Jehoshaphat *was at peace*, for his God gave him rest *on all sides.*"

We begin with a man being afraid and end with him being at rest. Between this beginning and ending something happened. Knowing that all Scripture is "profitable for teaching . . . for training in righteousness . . . or edification," let's explore the secret of Jehoshaphat's success in turning his heart into the faith-rest life.

Reports filtered in that a massive army from three different nations were surrounding Jehoshaphat with every intention of conquering Israel. Little wonder he was fearful. The uncertainty of not knowing what was going to happen next; the insecurity and lack of safety; the bewilderment about what to do and how to do it, are ripe emotions in which fear grows and multiplies. What he did will be the major discussion, but first some things about fear.

FEAR CAN BE A PAST PRODUCT

These armies had no right to be there. In fact, they shouldn't have existed at all. They were born of Lot's illegal children by his daughters during an act of foolish unbelief. A time when they didn't believe that God would take care of them. During such a time his daughters got him drunk and then impregnated themselves by him, fearful they wouldn't have any children to carry on their heritage.

The sons born of this unholy act became the fathers of the nations of these three armies now confronting Jehoshaphat and the nations of Israel. Our *fears today are usually the results of wrong believing yesterday.* Wrong acting and wrong outcomes lie buried deep in the rubbish of unbelief, and oft times disobedience. Fear is something that is left over from some previous event.

As such, these enemies shouldn't have been there, but they were. Had Lot's children not acted so fearfully they would have been nonexistent, but here they are, and had to be dealt with—now! Will this enemy terrify them? Cause them to cower before them? Will they dwarf them into doubting God's Word to protect them? Will they be intimidated into bringing reproach on their testimony that they are the children of the living God? Will their God take care of them now? It never was a question of whether God could, but would He? Every neighboring nation knew about the God of Israel, and not one of them doubted His ability to defend Israel, but like every unbeliever, they gambled on whether He would. Perhaps the most potent unbelief in existence is, "Well, I know God can, but I don't know if He will!" That is the basis of fear!

TWO POSITIVE FORCES

Both fear and faith are powerful emotions controlling

every aspect of life. You are what your faith or fear is, exactly that and nothing more. Because they are such powerful, influential forces, we are guided by them whether we want to be or not. The difference is which one you allow to dominate your life; will you practice the law of faith or the law of fear?

Jesus explained these two forces. Often He said, "Fear not, only believe!" (Luke 8:50), showing that these emotional forces are both positive and effective. The only way to overcome the force of fear is by the higher force of faith. It's like light and darkness. Light is stronger than darkness because light is a manifestation of energy, while darkness is not. Darkness is a force but not energy. It has no manifestation, only the absence of light. What happens when darkness enters a place filled with light? The light doesn't become darkness; rather the darkness is overpowered by the light. It disappears!

But when you turn a light on in a dark room what happens? The darkness vanishes and the whole room is bathed with light, manifested energy. That is because light is a stronger force than darkness.

So you see, fear is a force, but not energy. Faith is stronger than fear, being both a force and a manifestation of energy. It is a release of the Word and presence of God in you. Faith is both a fruit of the Spirit (Galatians 5:22) and a gift of God (I Corinthians 12:9). As a gift, it is energy; as a fruit, it is manifestation. Faith is a product of man trusting in God, while fear is the product of man doubting God.

Likewise, both faith and fear believe. Does that strike you as strange? Fear believes that God might fail, He won't get there on time. He can, but He might not . . . 180 degrees apart is faith which firmly confesses, God will! Fear is based on what your senses dictate, while faith operates on the Word of God. Man's senses, his intellect, emotions and will can fail while faith is based on God's Word which *cannot fail!*

Fear believes very actively in failure, while faith believes in success.

In Job 3:25 he said, "The thing I feared has come upon me," and his friends agreed with him (4:6). He believed that and it reduced him to an ash heap. Only when his believing and acting changed was he lifted.

Fear is the frustration, the inner conflict, that believes the problem can't be solved. Hell is filled with believers. They were believers who left God out of their thinking and living. They believed that He wasn't necessary for their happiness so they acted on that belief. When the Bible says that there will be "weeping, gnashing of teeth and wailing," it is simply detailing those frustrations, insecurities, and fears that have reached maturity. Oh, the bitter tears of remorse, now that it's too late, over what might have been. Tears spilled, mourning the impossibility of retrieving something precious, an active faith in God.

I wonder how many are now living in a similar hell? They're afraid of getting sick, afraid to die, fearful they'll go broke, fearful they'll stay poor, afraid they'll fail (don't worry they will!), afraid of criticism, of not being accepted, of enemies within and without, afraid of darkness, backsliding and yes, afraid of demons lurking under every bush. You name it; there's somebody that's afraid of it. Truly the way of the fearful is a hard path. They're believers, to be sure, real believers. They believe they're insecure and unsafe; therefore, they're fearful. More people actually practice a stronger belief in fear than in faith, which is foolish since we know that faith is a stronger force than fear.

It's our purpose in this chapter to take you from that fear into faith; from unrest into a rest that only God can give. While fear puts knots in the stomach, tenses the muscles, raises the blood pressure, and creates confusion, faith becomes a relaxing life-style. When Jesus emerged from Gethsemane after a night-long battle with hell itself, his own questions, and the will of God, he totally relaxed his disciples by telling them, "Let not your hearts be troubled. You believe in God, believe also in Me."

They undoubtedly heard the agonizing cries during the long, lonely vigil. Perhaps His "strong crying" unsettled them, though it is doubtful. They slept. Whether out of unconcern for His battle, or just knowing He'd win, I don't know. Still there must have been a sense of urgency among them. Otherwise, He wouldn't have told them, "Let not *your* hearts be troubled. I've got it settled now!" He imparted His peace to them, encouraging them for what was ahead. The conflict of that night wasn't removed, the cross still faced Him, but the momentary fear of it was. Peace reigned!

Let's return to Jehoshaphat, and how his fears became resting faith. There are at least four things he did that changed him and they can change you the same way: He changed his thinking, he changed his believing, he put actions into his thinking and believing, and he developed a faith image.

All of this was accomplished through praise, which mobilized his faith for action. In understanding this principle of praise let me point out that there isn't any evidence he thanked God for these enemies. Neither did he sit back waiting for something to happen. Neither Bible faith nor praise is passive acceptance, but militant resisting and receiving. Had he thanked God for his enemies and did nothing, it would have been another defeat for Israel. He followed a course that will work for you, too.

HE CHANGED HIS THINKING

He entered into God's presence by exalting Him (v. 6), which is always the first step. "Enter His gates with thanksgiving, and His courts with praise" (Ps. 100:4). In Isaiah 60:18 we read, "His walls are salvation and His gates are praise." In other words, man shouldn't come into the presence of God whinning, whimpering or crying, but boldly, with praise and thanksgiving. But how can a man do that when his heart is filled with fear? How can he praise God when he's hopeless, helpless, and confused? That's the reason we are to do it the Bible way. God knows exactly what we need!

Man's problem is the fear problem, manifested through his senses. What we're doing is changing that into a positive, stronger force called faith. So Jehoshaphat said, "O Lord, the God of our fathers, art thou not God in the heavens? And art thou not ruler over all the kingdoms of the nations? Power and might are in Thy hand so that no one can stand against Thee. Didst Thou not, O our God, drive out the inhabitants of this land before Thy people Israel, and give it to the descendants of Abraham Thy friend forever?" (2 Chron. 20:6,7).

What is God saying?

REPLACING EMOTIONAL FEAR WITH FAITH WORDS

By recalling the *past* victories of the Lord among His people, Jehoshaphat is overcoming his immediate fear. He's replacing emotional fears with faith words. It's like telling himself, "We've been tried and tested by the best and the biggest. Who do these Johnny-come-latelys think they are? We won before and we'll win again! By the way Lord, *if* anything drastic should happen to us, who will be left to praise thee, these people?"

Those are faith-filled words. By magnifying the Lord, a type of *HALAL,* he is honoring God. This is always the surest way to get into His presence. Those who come to Him must believe that He is and that he is a rewarder of those who diligently seek Him (Heb. 11:6). Attempting to approach God any other way is not the way of faith. Regardless of the magnitude of your problem, the only way to approach Him is by faith, and this never includes fear, doubt, unbelief or uncertainty. We must believe *that He is a reward-er of those who diligently seek Him!*

By thanking Him for *past* victories our faith is set up for immediate deliverance by overpowering the lesser force of fear. Jehoshaphat didn't mention his fears, but he did rejoice in the power of God, and he confessed it audibly. Even though his initial reaction was fear, his true confidence was in the Lord's enablement.

Notice also that this confidence wasn't necessarily a personal one. He mentions the Abrahamic covenant, the deliverance from the wilderness, and the original entering of Canaan, their inheritance. He wasn't there so what is he standing on? The Word of God, exactly the same foundation you and I can stand on. It was the record of the Lord's accomplishments in times *past,* and the promise that He would *never* forsake His people, including us.

How can anyone, you and I included, stay small, defeated, whimpering, and defeated when you're exalting the Lord? By magnifying and extolling the power of the Lord, Jehoshaphat didn't change God one whit, *but it sure changed him!* Had he voiced his fears they would have grown to the place where it would have been impossible to please God. So he uncluttered his mind by thinking about the Lord.

There isn't anything Satan fears more than a praising saint! There isn't *any* way he can get to them. His only means of testing is through the mental processes and when they are filled with God-exalting praises and faith-filled words, then he stands on the outside filled with fear. He knows from the beginning he's defeated as far as you're concerned; that's why he uses your emotions and intellect to frighten you. He's like a roaring lion, sneaking about, seeing who is available for him to devour. Don't you be one of them!

Further, it's imperative that you *identify your fears,* just as Jehoshaphat did. In verse 12 he said, "For we are powerless before this great multitude who are coming against us; nor do we know what to do, but our eyes are on Thee." Glory! You can't lose with a praise-confession like that! We're weak, powerless and afraid of being killed. And we don't know how to handle it. We're frustrated, discouraged and almost despondent. But our hope is in Thee, Lord God.

Voice those fears exactly as they are. Don't pretend they aren't there while you walk around, strutting with a swagger of victory, and everyone knows you've about had it. Don't try to act super-spiritual, at times presumptiously, but face them openly. No, this isn't negative confession, but an honest, positive one. Once you've delivered it to the Lord honestly, you won't have to confess it again.

FAITH'S VICTORY WILL OVERPOWER THAT LESSER FORCE

Then in verse 7 he brings to his own remembrance (it had to be for his benefit, God doesn't forget, nor does He need reminding), the covenant God made with Abraham, promising by an oath that this land would belong to his descendants forever. Now he's established a covenant relationship. A covenant is an agreement that cannot be broken, ever, for any reason, and God swore by Himself that the covenant would stand forever. This, without a doubt, established his faith on solid ground, the Word of God, and not what his senses told him. Part of that covenant promise was protection, and care when needed. All that was necessary was to stand in the place where the Lord dwelt, "and cry to Thee in our distresses, and Thou wilt hear and deliver us" (v.9).

Where does God dwell? In the praises of His people? How do we enter into that dwelling place? By thanksgiving and praise? Exactly!

Contrary to what some have been taught, the covenant promises given to Abraham are valid today and include everyone who is "in Christ" (Gal. 3:29). Therefore, the same

94

covenant ground that delivered Jehoshaphat from his enemies and fears will deliver us. For this we can shout, Glory!

Whenever I'm in trouble and need my faith quickened, I'm not going to passively settle down and accept what is happening as the will of God for me. Not when it disagrees with the covenant promises. I'll praise God that in the battle He will win; I'll praise and thank Him for *past* victories, and I'll stand on the covenant that the promises are mine and confess them before the Lord with *HALAL* and *TODAH*.

So Jehoshaphat knew how to get into God's presence. He *saw* God's people formed as a people of praise (Isa. 43:18), and he *saw* according to Deuteronomy 2:19-25 that the enemy wasn't supposed to be there at all, so why tolerate them?

HE CHANGED HIS BELIEVING

Jehoshaphat could have believed as the ten spies did at an earlier time, when they complained that the people of the land were too many. They were like giants and we, God's people, poor, defenseless and helpless, are like grass-hoppers. Or, he could have stood with 80-year-old Caleb when he boomed: "Those giants are the grasshoppers in the eyes of God, and I've got eyes like Him! I believe that we as a people are greater than they. Let's go get them!"

One spoke words of fear; the other words of faith. One pleased Satan; the other pleased God. One didn't know who they were; the other knew exactly who he was in God. One believes God meant what He said about giving them the land; the other sort of hopes so, thinks so, maybe believes so—it would be a nice gesture on His part wouldn't it?—or mentally agrees so, but never settles the issue.

It reminds me of the story about a man who was attempting a bicycle ride on a cable over Niagra Falls. Turning to an obviously enraptured lad in the crowd he asked him: "Son, do you think I'm able to ride this bike on this little cable over those falls?"

"Sure, I believe you can do it," the lad responded excitedly.

"Great! Get on and ride with me," he challenged.

From reddish, his complexion turned to white fear. "Yah, I believe maybe *you* can, but . . . let me see you do it first!"

Did he really believe or just thought he believed?

Watch Jehoshaphat progress from praise that led him into God's presence to presenting his problem. First there is praise, then there is prayer. Prayer, without the initial praise, is usually the whine of fear.

"Behold how they are rewarding us, by coming to drive us out from Thy possession which Thou has given us as an inheritance" (v. 11). What he's saying is: "Lord, they're trying to steal what is yours and you gave it to me, so it isn't mine, but yours, Lord." And therein is the key to successful battle with both men and fear. "Lord! take a look!"

He recognized that everything he had was a "gift" from God and received freely by grace. It was Jesus who emerged victor. It was Jesus who conquered Satan and stripped him of his usurped authority and gave it back to man at Calvary. It was Jesus who spoiled the spoiler, tasted death for us, tempted in all points as we are, suffered the pain of both sickness and death. For himself? Never! It was for you!

"When Jesus arose from the dead God freely gave Him all things, so that everything in heaven, on the earth and below the earth must bow their knees and confess that He is Lord to the glory of God" (Phil. 2:11, 12). But being the totally selfless one He is, He willingly shared that inheritance with each of us. So it's my inheritance but not really; it's His, shared with me eternally.

Likewise, the covenant inheritance Jehoshaphat spoke to God about was a promise between Abraham and God.

Yet he stood firmly on it. This was the problem. Those three armies withstanding Jehoshaphat weren't really confronting him, but God Himself. "Won't you judge them, Lord. We're powerless against them, but our eyes are on Thee" (v. 12).

How could God resist such total dependence? He couldn't avoid such a heart cry when He knew His name and inheritance was at stake. He couldn't, He will not forsake you for the same reason.

According to Colossians 1:13, we have been delivered from the authority of darkness, and everything involved with and in it, and already been delivered into the kingdom of His dear Son. That isn't something that's going to happen; it's final and finished! The tenses are *past* tense. We are *now* living in that kingdom of freedom, *which is our inheritance.* His inheritance which He willingly shares with us. "We are heirs and joint-heirs with Him" (Rom. 8:17).

So what does God do? He anoints a prophet in the camp by the name of Jahaziel who prophesies: "Listen, everyone, the Lord says this to you, don't be afraid, or dismayed because of this great multitude for the battle is not yours but the Lord's."

It's important that they be admonished again and again, don't be afraid! If you are, it will hinder anything God can do. He must have an atmosphere of praise, faith and active belief in order to move.

Has any word of the Lord ever returned to Him void? Never! His Word is His will, and His will must be accomplished, so as far as the Word is concerned, buckle your seat belts and hang on. When God declares a fact, why fear?

So what is happening now?

The *past* has been acknowledged and God honored it. Jehoshaphat's thinking has been changed.

Now the *present* is brought up. Their inheritance is at stake. They've confessed their desperate need and offered a sacrifice of thanksgiving for what they expect will happen.

They were changing their believing.

Believing is not a noun or mental act, but is a verb, that which denotes action. Thinking is mental and faith inspiring. Believing is acting on that thinking and is faith in action. It brings the distant into near focus.

After the Israelites had done this, things really began to happen. The Spirit of the Lord is in the camp. It's shouting time! When He's there and declares the battle is His and not ours, it is as good as over, I don't care how long He decides to play with it. It's this kind of praise that brings about the manifestation of the Spirit of God to edify and upbuild His people. This is what Paul meant when he said to "fight the good fight of faith," in 1 Timothy 6:12.

It's interesting to note that this prophet Jahaziel was from a long line of praisers. He was a direct relative of Mattaniah, the Levite of the sons of Asaph, one of David's original musicians who gave us many of the Psalms.

Their believing now says that God and His power is there to deliver. Nothing has happened yet, but they're already believing that it's done. No longer is there any evidence of fear or doubt remaining. They're standing on tiptoe waiting to see exactly how God works out this salvation for them, and again we see the Bible principle of the Word and faith in that Word. How much Scripture they actually had I don't know, but this I do know; they had the prophet of the Lord there. His word was the Word for them!

PRACTICING THE FAITH ATTITUDE THROUGH PRAISE

How much time has passed since the nation was called to prayer we aren't told, but one thing is obvious. Jehoshaphat isn't any longer afraid. "You need not fight in this battle; station yourselves, stand and see the salvation of the Lord on your behalf. Do not fear or be dismayed; tomorrow go out to face them, for the Lord is with you" (v. 17).

There's a wealth of information in that one verse.

• This isn't your battle but God's so let Him fight it. You can't conquer your own fears, and neither can psychiatrists, therapy, drugs or anything else. It's the Lord's battle. Only He can conquer those enemies.

• Station yourselves, stand and watch Him do it. When I was a little fellow, I didn't have a big brother to help me. Whenever a larger fellow decided to scrap with me (I was smaller than a normal boy, so easily picked on. I did, however, purposely have a big buddy who did watch out for me). I'd let the bigger fellow start it, get involved momentarily, then back off, go sit on the bank, while my buddy finished him off. I have the same protection working for me today. All I have to do is station myself in the Word, stand still, and watch Him work it out. Glory! Who needs to be afraid with a promise like that?

• That working is on your behalf. God doesn't do anything for Himself, but for you. So don't fear, or be dismayed!

• However, you must go out and face the enemy. Fears can never be overcome by hiding from them. No problem will ever go away of itself. Face that enemy, for the Lord is with you. Believe it! Then do it!

PRAISE IS FAITH IN ACTION

Please note now, the various attitudes and expressions of faith being exercised. (This chapter did more for me in helping me understand the real principles and power behind praise than any other in the Word. After I learned these the rest began to fit nicely together as a whole.)

Because Jehoshaphat was grateful, he humbled himself before the Lord by bowing his head and face to the ground (v. 18). This was in expression of *BARAK;* to prostrate oneself expecting to receive something. It was worship before the One who alone was worthy. Not only did he do this, but the whole nation with him.

Then in verse 19, the priests "Stood up to praise the

Lord God of Israel, with a very loud voice." The praise here is *HALAL*: To boast, magnify and glorify God. This is the substance of what the king had done in verse 6-8 when he entered the Lord's presence by audibly expressing the victories of God in the past.

We should note how they *HALALED*. "With a very loud voice." Kind of odd, isn't it? Wouldn't it frighten the enemy and make them aware of their attack? This is an expression of *SHABACH* which means to address God loudly, with a strong voice. What reasonable purpose is in this?

Most people, when gripped by fear, find an automatic release by screaming. You don't have to premeditate it; it's just there.

I recall once when I was driving the Pennsylvania Turnpike during the winter. I came from one side of a mountain where there was no snow at all. Then passing through a long tunnel I came out on the other side where there was snow everywhere. The plow had left a small pile of it right at the exit of the tunnel, and I hit it with a sudden thud doing about 60. Immediately I lost control and started spinning. Thankfully no one was behind me, but before I could even think I automatically hollered: "Jesus, help me!"

And He did! I hit a dry portion of the road and stopped as abruptly as I began spinning. That was *SHABACH*.

Can't you see that nation, most of them on their faces before God while the priests, with great dignity, decor and deportment, screamed their praises to God? The situation was desperate so why play church?

The next morning dawned with the sun rapidly rising on the misty horizon. I'm sure not too many slept well that night so mustering the people didn't require too much effort. Just before they left for the wilderness of Tekoa where they would confront the armies and just "stand still and see the salvation of God," Jehoshaphat exhorted them. Gave them a little pep-talk. "Listen to me O Judah and inhabitants of

100

Jerusalem, put your trust in the Lord your God, and you will be established. Put your trust in His prophets and succeed" (v. 20).

Simply amazing. For a man so fearful yesterday to talk like a lion today! What happened? He had praised the Lord, confessed the Word, and his doubts, unbeliefs and fears were swallowed up in the Word. His problem was still there but something greater and stronger than his problem overshadowed it. What he tells them is: "Trust in the Lord" and you'll be established in His promises. "Believe His prophets" and you'll succeed. It's the same formula from Genesis to maps: Believe God and stand on His Word! It's a winning combination!

Then calling certain of the people he placed them in position.

First and foremost would *not* be the soldiers, heavily armed and trained in natural warfare. This battle, being the Lord's, would not be fought with carnal weapons so the priests would lead them. "Those who praised the Lord in holy attire" (v. 21).

The word used for praise here is *YADAH;* to lift the hands in power. They were expressing their complete dependence on Him. Their hands said, "I need you, Lord, or I won't be here to praise you tomorrow!" In fact, their ministry was to praise the Lord this way. What an army! Priests, many of them, clothed with priestly garb, marching with raised arms, stretched to the heavens, leading along columns of Israelites. (I've always wondered what the reactions were when the enemy first spotted them? Who ever fought a war like this?)

Then they were, "Giving thanks to the Lord, for His loving-kindness is everlasting" (v. 21). "Thanks" here is *TOWDAH:* thanksgiving. And why were they doing this? Because they were believing that He *would* deliver according to their confession, and because His loving-kindness is everlasting.

Loving-kindness is a word frequently translated as mercy. This reason, above all others in the Bible, is given as the reason for praise of all kinds. His mercy, His loving-kindness, *is* everlasting. The Israelites realized this and depended strongly on it. This is drawing on His oaths, goodness, love, power, His very Person which is to *give!*

And now it gets exciting and revelationary.

"And *WHEN* they began singing *AND* praising, the Lord sent ambushments and the enemy was routed" (v. 22).

WHEN, WHEN, WHEN, they began singing. *AND, AND, AND* praising, the Lord intervened.

Everything thus far led up to this climatic moment. All the praising, changing of thinking and believing, of leaving behind the emotions of fear, led to this conclusion, the Lord intervened.

This is the single verse that revealed to me that *TEHILLAH* which means basically "to sing" was more than just singing. Scripture said, "and when they began singing *AND* praising. . . . " Two separate expressions but somehow tied together.

TEHILLAH is a derivative of *HALAL;* therefore, it was a boasting, magnifying, a glorifying God that was sung or chanted. Today we understand and practice it as "singing in the Spirit" (Eph. 5:19).

It was important that we discover the true understanding inasmuch as Psalm 22:3 states that God inhabits this particular kind of praise. It is where His Lordship is manifested; where He meets with man and where He is enthroned.

Apparently the "singing" in our text overcame what remained of their doubts, plus. They were joyfully expecting and believing. Something had to give! For such singing often flows into *TEHILLAH,* that praise in which God makes Himself known. Suddenly, He came just as expected. How?

Fear had been overpowered by the stronger force of

faith.

The people were unified through their singing. All negative talk was silenced by their joyful voices.

Every rebellious heart, if there were any, was brought into obedience to the Word of the Lord *when they sang and praised the Lord.* Vain imaginations were cast down; the timid spirit of the fearful was transformed into victorious believers, and the Lord was glorified. He had to come! Praise which is faith in action was irresistible!

THE VALLEY OF BERACHAH

When God comes on the scene making good His Word strange things can happen. We call them miracles, something placed in the natural world that can't be explained naturally. In this instance God caused three armies to get confused, and they caught each other in some sort of cross fire so that "they helped destroy one another" (v. 23). Details are lacking, because it took place *while* Jehoshaphat was still praising the Lord *for* the victory that *would* take place before it actually happened. (Doesn't that give the same content as what Jesus said in Mark 11:23?)

When they reached the lookout of the wilderness they looked down in the valley and corpses lay everywhere. Not a single one had escaped. Such total victory completely eliminated everything that had caused them fear. What remained but the memory of what could have been? And thus it is with us.

"God has not given you the spirit of fear, but of power, and of love, and of a sound mind" in Jesus Christ. Therefore, "cast down vain imaginations and every high thing that exalts itself against the Lord Jesus Christ, and bring every thought into captivity." Not an enemy can remain. "He who the Lord sets free *is* free indeed."

They stood high above the battlefield looking down on the wreckage, and saw what God had wrought. And it all took place while they were marching out to face the enemy with nothing to defend themselves except confidence in the Lord and praise on their lips. Such is the miracle of praise!

They spent the next three days cleaning up the spoils that were left behind, but on the fourth day they headed for Jerusalem, the city of God, *with joy,* for the Lord had caused them to rejoice over their enemies (v. 27).

"And the kingdom of Jehoshaphat *was at peace,* for his God gave him rest *on all sides*" (v. 30).

They won! And you can too!

Their general attitude was changed when they took knowledge of the living God, believed His Word and sang His praise (Psalm 106:12). All seven expressions of "praise" were used. Each serving a specific purpose; the whole man was involved, spirit, soul and body. It still works the same way today.

What happened to a handful of scared, fearful men who had been with the Lord for three and one-half years that changed them into a band of preachers who shook nations, disturbed demons, caused hell to quiver, and whose reputations preceeded them as "men who disturbed nations?"

It was their enthusiasm, matured in the presence of Jesus. The neighbors "took notice that they had been with Jesus." Fear had turned to faith.

Before Pentecost the disciples locked themselves behind closed doors lest they, too, be captured, tried and put to death as revolutionaries. But on the day of Pentecost, after praising the Lord for some ten days, the Spirit came and the enemies called fear, uncertainty and insecurity were routed. These enemies were turned against one another until they were completely annihilated. Something happened so drastic that one moment Peter is a coward and shortly thereafter his preaching wins 3,000 to the Lord amidst threats. Fear was overpowered by praise, and fear conquered by faith.

PRAISE AS A FAITH IMAGE

What Peter saw was the reality of a promise given them days before. Jesus said, "Ye shall be my witnesses in my stead. You'll do exactly as I've done and more. You'll take my place; use my name as your legal authority, but go! Do it! And I'll go with you! The battle isn't yours; but mine! I'll work with you with signs following. And Peter this isn't just for you, but for everyone who believes also. It will deliver anyone bound in the spirit of fear and deliver them into the power of faith."

They saw themselves as "take charge" men, and so are you. God's Spirit is power, love and a sound mind. His victory is complete. His provision is endless. You must, however, stand on it, stand with it, and see the Lord's salvation. It's for you!

And Jehoshaphat had peace in his kingdom.

So will you!

Chapter Eight

How to Win Over
and Withstand Your Enemy

"O Lord, our Lord, how majestic is Thy name in all the earth, Who hast displayed Thy splendor above the heavens! From the mouth of infants and nursing babes Thou hast established strength, because of Thine adversaries, to make the enemy and the revengeful cease" (Ps. 8:1-2 NAS).

How I rejoiced the first time I uncovered the gem hidden in this passage. For those of you who are like I was, caught up in periods of almost endless struggling, when nothing would give, the truth in this verse will liberate you.

With the current emphasis on demons and deliverance, this principle is like a breath of fresh air. At a minimum it's like preventive medicine and the only alternative for maintaining deliverance, but it's more, much more. It provides the needed strength to withstand the frontal attacks of the enemy which includes anything that hinders my maturing process and my fellowship with the Father and His Son, Christ Jesus.

Unless this passage is compared with other scriptures it's meaning is nearly lost but note in your margin the reference to Matthew 21:16 and turn there with me.

This was the last journey Jesus would make into Jerusalem on what we now refer to as Palm Sunday. His disciples provided an unbroken donkey, and unbeknown to them,

Jesus began that eternal journey to Calvary. He knew who He was and what He was doing, but like so many today, those around Him were oblivious to that.

Everyone was caught up in the excitement. Both adults and children ran before Him, paving the little animal's path with palm branches and shouting, "Hosanna to the Son of David; blessed is He who comes in the name of the Lord; Hosanna in the highest!" According to the account this caused quite a stir, especially among the religionists. No one had ever been afforded such an exuberant welcome, not even their high priest, and what right did this self-styled prophet possess to receive such an ovation? Later that day when He healed all that came to him, the blind, the lame and the crippled, without their permission, they agreed among themselves that He must be corrected.

"Why don't you rebuke them" they charged Jesus. "They're calling you the Son of David. Can't you hear what they're saying?"

Little children crowded around Him, eager for His touch. "Hosanna to the highest" they cried. Soon, no one could hear anything except their intoxicating shouting.

A slight grin appeared at the corners of His bronzed face. Looking at them intently, yet with understanding eyes, He replied, "Yes, and haven't you read, 'out of the mouths of infants and nursing babes Thou hast prepared praise for Thyself?' " Turning He walked away, leaving them stinging from His near insult. After all, weren't they the students and knew more about the scriptures than any other sect in Israel? How dare He say, "Haven't *you* read?" While they pondered His words, He proceeded to heal others. Yes, they had read those words of the psalmist, but like so many today, they didn't understand them. Neither had I, and then I saw the truth!

What the psalmist called "established strength" the Master called "prepared" or "prepared praise." Surely Jesus wouldn't have altered the meaning of the two passages nor taken them out of context. Obviously there was a vital connection. In the margin of the NAST is the word "bulwark" which adds a possible thought. Established strength may be or comes from "established bulwarks" or strong walls of defense, and this Jesus said comes from "prepared praise." Could it be that God both protects His "little ones" as well as matures them so that their praise may result in His glory?

Infants and babes must grow through exercising every faculty of their body through trial and error. For example: is there a baby alive who ever learned that a hot stove wasn't to be touched except through the painful lesson of touching? Therefore, praise must be a vehicle through which we can mature, thereby causing our enemies and adversaries to quit their activities. If this established strength is directly linked to the maturing process, then I need it. Since that time I've learned in one area of Christian living after another, that the truth and principle of this verse is workable. For example: I've learned to trust Him for finances through praise and at first it was rough.

My first church paid me exactly $25 a week without any benefits. Out of that I paid $10 a week auto payment. Need I mention that often that salary was spent before I received it, but Glad and I learned how to trust Him. We'd lay before the Lord exactly what was needed and begin offering to Him the sacrifice of thanksgiving long before the actual money was there, but we knew one thing. He had obliged Himself, through His Word, to meet those needs so we didn't doubt for a moment that He would.

First we grew strong trusting Him for gas money, then other extras. Never, since we entered into this ministry have we been broke. We've been badly bent a few times, but never completely without funds. As each conflict was overcome we were stronger than before. In the beginning, believing Him

108

for $25 seemed like a huge mountain, but now, years later, we believe for thousands of dollars yearly, knowing for certain the needs will always be met.

How can we be so certain?

Because we've been through the steps, one by one, we've established strength, we've built a strong bulwark, a defense that is sure. We're safely behind that wall of strength and assurance. Jesus is that wall, He is the source of strength in that wall, and He is behind that wall with us.

Our text declares that such strength, once established, will make the enemy and avenger cease. They'll quit trying after a while. He'll wander around in circles looking for an opening, looking for a stone that hasn't been established yet. A promise that hasn't been proven. If he finds it, he'll immediately begin his invasion and robbery of your inheritance at that point. That's when you begin a new adventure into the praise-faith life and secure that place. Once you've securely laid that particular stone he'll quit and begin his endless searching for a weak place.

That scriptural promise, that next step towards maturity, must be tested before it is yours. Before that, the promises are exactly that, promises. But after you've established strength through prepared praise, they are no longer promises but realities.

If you want this available ability, this source of strength, you'll have to learn how by doing. This aspect of praise is possibly the most powerful weapon provided for God's warrior children. But remember, as K. Hagin has said, "This is no nine-inning ball game, bless God, I play until I win." With an attitude like that strength will soon be yours.

According to this text (1) we're dealing with the source of established strength, the how and it's development, the building of a strong wall of defense; (2) its function as a stabilizing factor already provided in every child of God, regardless of their state of maturity; and (3) its use as an offensive weapon that will route the enemy (which includes all direct encounters) and the revengeful (those indirect attacks from within).

This is what Jesus had in mind when He stated that the praise He received looked forward to the grounds for the "little ones" strength and protection. He was on His way to the cross, death, hell and Satan's final defeat. Throughout His entire earthly ministry Jesus continually entered the "strong man's house" in order to eventually spoil him, take away his armour and source of strength, and distribute the plunder (see Luke 11:20-22). Because Satan, the enemy and adversary of God, had reduced man to a puppet through sin and death, Jesus, of necessity, met him frontally in the arena of faith and stripped away any control and authority Satan held over man.

He became sin so that we may be made righteous.

He was tempted in all ways we are, yet without yielding, so that we may be victorious.

He was made sick so that we can be well.

He, though rich, became poor, so that we, who are poor, may be made rich.

Though He was strong, He became weak, so that we may be strong.

He was condemned, rejected and despised by ignorant men, so that we may be accepted of the Father.

He died so that we may live. He entered hell, wherever and whatever, so that we may enter the heavenlies. He submitted to the legalism of dead religion so that we may be free to worship in spirit and in truth.

Whatever Satan put upon mankind Jesus took away by taking it on Himself. Whatever Satan put in mankind He took out, and every thing he took away from man, Jesus restored back to him again. He did all this, and more, not for Himself, but for you, the "little ones." The bite of sin and sting of death were removed, and today Satan stands as God's "toothless wonder," a memorial of the total victory of Jesus. Now, because Jesus lives we live also, so why stand around letting Satan gum you?

That's what Jesus had in mind when He quoted Psalm 8:2 in Matthew 21:16. He knew, but those around Him were as unaware of His mission as most living people today (1 John 3:8).

Turn to 1 Peter 1:6 and read with me: "In this you greatly rejoice, even though now for a little while, if necessary, you have been distressed by various trials."

Does that sound familiar to you? If you're not having any battles, just hold steady. It won't be long before Elijah's chariot will soon remove you from our midst. Meanwhile, the rest of us have those battles which become our opportunities to win.

"That the proof of your faith, being more precious than gold which is perishable, even though tested by fire, may be found to result in praise and glory and honor at the revelation of Jesus Christ" (1 Pet. 1:7).

Now there's some guarantee. At least these incessant confrontations are proving my faith with a definite, God-ordained purpose. That is if you know where you're going and don't cave in along the way. By proving your faith, they establish a strength that is more endurable than refined gold, resulting in "prepared praise" for Him. In other words, those fiery testings aren't to defeat or overpower you, but to establish you. God doesn't try us to find out our weak points but to establish our strong ones. Religion spends much of its time pointing out man's weaknesses, which God has already delegated as totally worthless, while the Word seeks to establish you in strength by pointing out Christ's strength which is really yours.

How can anyone trust God as long as they're able to make it on their own? Anyone can say they trust Him for their daily bread when their cupboard is filled. Anyone can vocally declare their trust in His healing power when they're well, but what comes out of their mouth when they're sick? Is that the time you dig that "just-in-case" medical insurance policy? Everything pertaining to godliness and holy living has been provided. Everything needed to establish you in faith is yours, but it must be proved. No, not to God, He already knows what you'll do, but to yourself. You don't know what you'll do. Therefore, He sets you up. He allows these testing times, yes, He ordains them. Knowing that I can enter any battle with my winning guaranteed, I don't mind losing a few battles along the way. Oh, I know that I'll have to play that inning until I win, but the victory is assured. The last page of the contract says, "My side wins!"

Peter continues: ". . . and though you have not seen Him, you love Him, and though you do not see Him now, but believe in Him, you greatly rejoice with joy inexpressible and full of glory, obtaining as the outcome of your faith the salvation of your souls" (vs. 6-9).

Do you see it? Regardless of the conflict, when it is fought with God's weapons, praise-faith, the result is sure victory. A guaranteed victory, I might add.

Instead of complaining, try praising. Rather than talk negatively, fill your mouth with positive praise. Instead of copying the adult, mature Pharisees, who refused to praise the King, act like the "infants and nursing babes" and extoll the Lord of Glory. The results are guaranteed. Learn how to praise the Lord realizing it is faith in action, and then live in total victory.

The key is: They believed His Word, then they sang His praise!

Appendix

Fourteen Ways To Praise The Lord Biblically

1. PRAISE WHICH CAN BE HEARD

"O bless our God, ye people, and *make the voice of His praise to be heard"* (Ps. 66:8).

"I cried unto him with my mouth, and *he was extolled with my tongue"* (Ps. 66:17).

"Make a joyful noise unto the Lord, all the earth: make a loud noise, and rejoice, and sing praise" (Ps. 98:4).

"And at midnight Paul and Silas prayed, and sang praises unto God, and the prisoners heard them" (Acts 16:25).

There doesn't seem to be any Bible evidence that anyone ever praised the Lord silently in their hearts. It was always vocal and could be heard.

2. PRAISE THE LORD WITH SHOUTING

"O clap your hands, all ye people; shout unto God with the voice of triumph" (Ps. 47:1).

"Let them shout for joy and rejoice, who favor my vindication" (Ps. 35:27 NAS).

"O come, let us sing for joy to the Lord; let us shout joyfully to the rock of our salvation" (Ps. 95:1 NAS).

There are many passages where the psalmists urged everyone to shout unto the Lord with the voice of victory.

3. PRAISE HIM WITH SINGING

"Sing praises to God, sing praises; sing praises unto our King, sing praises" (Ps. 47:6).

There are countless scriptures that show singing as one of

the main forms of praise.

4. PRAISE YOUR LORD WITH THANKSGIVING
"I will praise the name of God with a song, and will magnify him with thanksgiving" (Ps. 69:30).

"He who offers a sacrifice of thanksgiving honors Me" (Ps. 50:23 NAS).

"I will sacrifice unto thee with the voice of thanksgiving" (Johah 2:9).

Next to singing praise, thanksgiving is the expression most understood. "In everything give thanks" the apostle Paul exhorts in Ephesians 5:18-20.

5. PRAISE GOD WITH A JOYFUL NOISE
"Make a joyful noise unto God . . . make His praise glorious" (Ps. 66:1, 2).

"Let us shout joyfully to the rock of our salvation" (Ps. 95:1 NAS).

God's people have always been a happy sort even when circumstances warrant otherwise. Regardless, they can *teruwah* = clamour, acclamation of joy.

6. PRAISE HIM WITH CRYING OUT
"Cry out and shout, thou inhabitant of Zion: for great is the Holy One of Israel in the midst of thee" (Isa. 12:6).

"He shall cry unto me, Thou art my Father, my God, and the rock of my salvation" (Ps. 89:26).

No, it isn't irreligious, or lacking in dignity to loudly and vocally express your joy and love to your Father.

7. PRAISE THE LORD WITH LAUGHTER
Read the whole of Psalm 126, especially verse 2, Then our mouth was filled with laughter, and our tongue with joyful shouting. This isn't laughing trivially, but with pure joy.

8. PRAISE WITH MUSICAL INSTRUMENTS

"Praise the Lord with harp" (Ps. 33:2).

"Awake up, my glory; awake, psaltery and harp" (Ps. 57:8).

Praise Him according to Psalm 150, where no less than eight different instruments are named.

9. PRAISE GOD BY BOWING AND KNEELING BEFORE HIM

"O come, let us worship and bow down: let us kneel before the Lord our maker" (Ps. 95:6).

". . . I bow my knees unto the Father of our Lord Jesus Christ" (Eph. 3:14).

". . . every knee should bow . . . and every tongue confess that Jesus Christ is Lord, to the glory of God the father" (Phil. 2:10, 11).

10. PRAISE HIM BY FALLING PROSTRATE BEFORE HIM

"And Ezra blessed the Lord, the great God. And all the people answered, Amen, Amen, with lifting up their hands; and they bowed low their heads, and worshipped the Lord with their faces to the ground" (Neh. 8:6).

11. PRAISE WITH CLAPPING THE HANDS

"O clap your hands, all ye people" (Ps. 47:1).

"Let the floods clap their hands" (Ps. 98:8).

In every area of life, clapping the hands is an expression of approval, excitement, and pure joy. Should it be otherwise when praising our Lord? Not according to Scripture. This is another area where the tradition of the elders has made null and void the commandments of God.

12. YOU CAN PRAISE HIM WITH UPLIFTED HANDS

"Thus will I bless thee while I live: I will lift up my hands in thy name" (Ps. 63:4).

"Lift up your hands in the sanctuary, and bless the Lord" (Ps. 134:2).

". . . and the lifting up of my hands as the evening offering" (Ps. 141:2).

13. PRAISE GOD WITH THE DANCE

"Thou hast turned for me my mourning into dancing" (Ps. 30:11).

"Let them praise his name in the dance" (Ps. 149:3).

"Praise him with the . . . dance" (Ps. 150:4).

Dancing, as described by the psalmists, was more of a rejoicing jump than one of grace. David danced before the Lord with all his might (2 Sam. 6:14).

14. PRAISE THE LORD WITH TONGUES

"For they heard them speak with tongues, and magnify God" (Acts 10:46).

"Otherwise if you bless in the spirit only, how will the one who fills the place of the ungifted say the 'Amen' at your giving of thanks, since he does not know what you are saying. For you are giving thanks well enough, but the other man is not edified" (I Cor. 14:16, 17).

One obvious fact throughout this praise study is that no one is exempt. Let everything that has breath praise the Lord. In fact, there is only one kind of person who doesn't praise the Lord as we've outlined from the word of God: THE DEAD DO NOT PRAISE THE LORD!

So come alive! Put your faith into action! Enter into the praise life!

BOOKS BY
CHARLES TROMBLEY

KICKED OUT OF THE KINGDOM $1.75

The thrilling account of a series of miracles that led a Jehovah's Witness family into Christianity. A best-seller and excellent reading for those who doubt modern miracles.

BIBLE ANSWERS FOR JEHOVAH WITNESSES. 2.00

There's strength in knowledge, so learn how to effectively handle most false teachings with confidence. Answers, not only for Jehovah's Witnesses, but most cults.

VISITATION – THE KEY TO CHURCH GROWTH 75

Written with Gordon Lindsay suggesting an effective plan for sharing your faith through gifts, faith, and hard work. A must for Christian workers.

BOOKLETS:. 35
WHAT HAPPENED TO THE BODY OF JESUS?
THE HOLY SPIRIT – WHO?
WHO IS THIS OTHER JESUS?

(These studies were written especially for Jehovah's Witnesses.)

Comments, inquiries or requests for speaking engagements, catalog, books, or cassette-teaching tapes should be directed to:

Charles Trombley Ministries
500 N. Elm Place
Broken Arrow, Okla. 74012

QUAN.	TITLE	PRICE

1FS   **VICTORY THROUGH FAITH**   **15.00** ....
.... **SERIES (6 tapes)**
Practical studies shared to make your faith come alive.

F100   **AUTHORITY OF JESUS' NAME**   **3.00** ....
.... Learn it's power, meaning, how obtained and when given. Cause hell to shudder, sickness to flee and demons to scatter.

F101   **HOW TO EXERCISE YOUR FAITH**   **3.00**
.... Hebrews 11 taught by principles relating to degrees of faith. Discover the seven ways to increase your faith and the five conditions for releasing it.

F102   **PRAISE IS FAITH AT WORK**   **3.00** ....
.... The force of faith is a combination of belief, confession and thanksgiving. Learn from Psalm 50 the greatest force known to man and how the force of faith can be released.

F103   **AUTHORITY OF THE WORD**   **3.00** ....
.... Basic to any faith. God's Word is His will and purpose. To doubt it is to doubt God Himself, thus the basis for Satan's attacks.

F104   **YOUR WORDS ARE**   **3.00** ....
.... **LIFE AND HEALTH**
Or sickness and death. Learn the power of words and some things never to confess.

F106   **FAITH THAT FUNCTIONS**   **3.00** ....
.... From James 2 we discover that faith must have corresponding actions. Making your actions agree with God's Word is what this study is about.

2FS   **TRIAL OF YOUR FAITH**   **7.50**
.... **SERIES (3 cassettes)**   ....
Faith without works is dead faith, good for nothing, Trials won't increase your faith so why the trials?

F105   **WHY SOME CHRISTIANS**   **3.00**
.... **AREN'T HEALED**   ....
Have you ever been sick, stood on the Word, confessed positively, praised and yet remained sick? What happened? This message is for you!

F107   **WHY YOUR FAITH DOESN'T**   **3.00**
.... **WORK (NEW)**   ....
Where does time fit into the faith walk if at all? A reexamination of Hebrews 11 that will benefit you.

F108   **WHY GOD ALLOWS**   **3.00**
.... **PROLONGED TRIALS (NEW)**   ....
Lessons from the book of Job in the light of the faith walk which result in both increased faith as well as greater blessings. Understand the trial of Job.

3HSS   **HOLY SPIRIT SERIES**
.... **(Individual messages)**
An apologetic series dealing with charismatic phenomena and objections to it.

HS100   **DISPENSATIONALISM VS.**   **3.00** ....
.... **THE BAPTISM**
Have spiritual gifts ceased? Did we receive the baptism when we were saved? Insights into the arguments used to reject the charismatic renewal.

HS101   **WHAT GOOD ARE TONGUES?**   **3.00** ....
.... Exactly what is the meaning and purpose of tongues? Are they an end or the launching pad into something greater? 19 reasons given for tongues.

HS102   **THE WHOLE CHRIST #1**   **3.00** ....
.... This is a study of the three Greek words for "gifts" showing how the nine gifts, the nine fruit, and nine governments constitute the Whole Body.

HS103   **THE WHOLE CHRIST #2**   **3.00** ....
.... **(continued)**
The interdependent relationships of the multiple ministries is shown as One New Man, THE WHOLE CHRIST.

QUAN.	TITLE	PRICE

HS104 **HOW TO HEAR AND TEST** 3.00 ....
.... PROPHECY—Side 1
AIDS TO PROPHESYING—Side 2
Prophecy as an expression of the Spirit must be understood,
sought and judged. Scriptural steps are suggested for flowing in
prophecy. Some guidelines for judging prophecy are given.

HS105 **1967 IN PROPHECY** 3.00 ....
.... Joel's prophecy was to be fulfilled simultaneously with an out
pouring of the Spirit universally. Beginning with the Dispersion of
Israel the exact chronology is worked out climaxing with the "6
Day War" and the Charismatic Renewal. An exciting, revealing
message on actual prophecy fulfilled in your lifetime.

4KG **KINGDOM OF GOD SERIES** 10.00 ....
.... **(4 cassettes)**
Every believer wants to do God's will and relate to His plan for
their lives. This series clearly shows the difference between the
Kingdom that now is and the Kingdom that is coming.

K100 **INTRODUCTION TO THE KINGDOM** 3.00 ....
.... What motivated early believers that enabled them to shake the
world? An unfolding of the what, where and when of God's
Kingdom today.

K101 **THE GOSPEL OF THE** 3.00 ....
.... **KINGDOM**
What was the "good news" Jesus preached? A study into
"Jubilee" as it relates to us personally. What are the "keys"
Jesus gave to Peter?

K102 **THE MYSTERIES OF THE** 3.00 ....
.... **KINGDOM**
A comparative, illuminating study between Matthew 13 and Rev.
2-3 as the Kingship of Jesus is gradually replaced by humans.

K105 **ESTABLISHING THE** 3.00 ....
.... **KINGDOM**
Romans 14:12 says the kingdom is righteousness, peace and joy.
We are able ministers of that spirit and kingdom. Learn how to
minister the Christ to others as we become Christ-like.

5KG **KINGDOM LIVING SERIES** 12.50 ....
.... **(5 cassettes)**
Knowing about the Kingdom and entering in are two different
things. If you find it difficult to get started this series will
stimulate your faith into a fruitful, fulfilling life.

K109 **HAS THE KINGDOM BEEN** 3.00 ....
.... **POSTPONED? (NEW)**
Contrary to a popular Bible it hasn't! Take an in depth look into
their arguments postponing the Kingdom for the millennium and
the Jews only.

K103 **PURPOSE OF DISCIPLESHIP** 3.00 ....
.... **(NEW)**
Both Martha and Mary were discipled by Jesus yet one failed
miserably during a test. She had't learned Who Jesus was. What
made the difference? The answer could save you many
heartaches.

K104 **MINISTERING UNTO GOD** 3.00 ....
.... Learn when god took a new people for His nation, made them a
Kingdom who would minister unto Him. Understand the place of
praise in the Kingdom.

K105 **LET'S POSSESS OUR** 3.00 ....
.... **INHERITANCE**
You have a possession in Christ, but the entrance is blocked by
several common enemies. Discover who they are and how to
claim every foot that is yours.

K107 **KINGDOM MINISTRY AND** 3.00 ....
.... **POWER**
We taste the powers of the world to come in the same measure
we function in Kingdom authority. Learn how to lay hold of that
dominion by confession and an attitude of gratitude.

QUAN.	TITLE	PRICE

6PS **WORKSHIP IN PRAISE** 7.50 ....
.... **SERIES (3 cassettes)**
There is more to praise than just saying. "PTL." Learn why God doesn't need your praise as much as you need to praise Him.

P100 **ART OF PRAISE** 3.00 ....
.... An actual workshop on "how" to praise the Lord. Learn the motions of praise and singing in the spirit. Discover God's plan for release of your inhibitions.

P101 **APPLICATION OF** 3.00 ....
.... **PRAISE #1**
How to approach God through praise. Praise (1) Enthrones Emmanuel. (2) is the Way into His Presence. (3) the Status of the Saints and (4) the Power of His Presence.

P102 **APPLICATION OF** 3.00 ....
.... **PRAISE #2**
Praise is (5) Faith that Functions. (6) Available Ability. and (7) Conquers Circumstances. Some common hindrances to faith are given. .

7CUL **CULT SERIES**
.... **(Individual lessons)**
With false religions abounding. due mainly to lack of knowledge about them, these teachings are imperative reading for those who would defend the faith against their subversive doctrines.

C100 **JEHOVAH'S WITNESSES AND JESUS** 3.00 ....
.... **DEITY Side 1 (NEW)**
IS JESUS MICHAEL THE ARCHANGEL?
Side 2
Why they deny His deity; how they reduce Him to an angel; why they reject His total Lordship. A complete refutation.

DEB1 **DEBATE WITH A JEHOVAH'S** 3.00 ....
.... **WITNESS. (NEW)**
An actual confrontation with an experienced Witness. Humurous and enlightening.

DEB2 Debate continued.

CL1 **THE MARKS OF CULTISM** 3.00 ....
.... **(NEW)**
Understanding the common denominators. motivation. basic doctrines of all cults.

R100 **KICKED OUT OF THE** 3.00 ....
.... **KINGDOM**
The miraculous intervention of God in the Trombley family resulting in untold numbers of Witnesses finding their way into the light of Christianity.

8CBN **UNDERSTANDING CULTISM** 7.50• ....
.... **(3 cassettes)**
A total of five half-hour broadcasts filmed for the Christian Broadcasting Network covering the entire cult problem.

CBN1 **THE CHRISTIAN AND THE CULTS** 3.00 ....
.... **Side 1 (NEW)**
CULT BASICS Side 2
From 1 Tim. 3:16- 4:16 the work of seducing spirits is understood as denying Jesus' Lordship. Both positive and negative factors are discussed, and a listing of the major cults are named.

CBN2 **WHAT HAPPENS TO A CULTIST** 3.00 ....
.... **SPIRITUALLY? Side 1 (NEW)**
THE CULTS AND JESUS Side 2
Leadership. extra-local authority. extra-Biblical revelations. structural control and exclusivism are explained as total mind control. This leads into side 2 and their views concerning the Lord Jesus. Every modern cult opinion about Jesus is revealed in the light of ancient heresies.

CBN3 **ANTIDOTE TO CULTISM (NEW)** 3.00 ....
.... The place of the Word, final revelation, and active faith are laid out as heaven's counterinvasion.

QUAN.	TITLE	PRICE

9MAR   **MARRIAGE RELATIONSHIP**   **7.50** ....
.... **SERIES (3 cassettes)**
What every man should know about their wives. Given at a men's retreat for the FGBMFI and extremely effective.

MAR100   **MALE AND FEMALE MADE**   **3.00** ....
.... **HE THEM (NEW)**
Contrary to current thought made them different. Beginning with Eden the marriage trail is traced with obvious lessons outlined. Humorous but true.

MAR101   **WHY WOMEN REACT LIKE**   **3.00** ....
.... **THEY DO. (NEW)**
A continuation of MAR100 but sharing "secrets" learned over 25 years of marriage and observation. Why women are emotional while men are coldly logical.

MAR102   **HOW TO LOVE YOUR WIFE**   **3.00** ....
.... **THE JESUS WAY. (NEW)**
Will bring out every God given response in her but how to love her

10WA   **UNDERSTANDING GOD'S**   **12.50** ....
.... **WAYS (5 cassettes)**
A camp meeting special focusing on the dealings of God in bringing the believer into full fellowship and maturity.

L100   **WHATCHA DOIN' GOD?**   **3.00** ....
.... Can I really know God? Yes, but unless we know the principles He uses in bringing it about we'll always ask, "Why did you do that God?" And end up fighting His ways.

L101   **FOLLOW THE LEADER**   **3.00** ....
.... Submitting to His ways must be personally learned as He deals with every person differently. Learn the steps to submission through confession, living faith, obedience, listening to His voice and teaching others His ways.

L102   **ACCEPTING HIS WAYS**   **3.00** ....
.... A continuation of L101. One may see the principles involved without willingly accepting them. You'll say "yes" to God easier after this message.

L103   **LEARNING DEPENDENCE**   **3.00** ....
.... Man's real problem is independence. Therefore dependence is learned as our temperaments are brought into conflict. Questions are asked that will help you determine why you react as you do.

L104   **KNOW YOUR ENEMIES**   **3.00** ....
.... Canaan is a type of our inheritance with Christ. The seven enemies who withstood all who would possess the land are studied as spiritual forces. Once you see yourself as God sees you you'll utterly slay the enemy.

11RD   **REDEMPTION SERIES**   **7.50** ....
.... **(3 cassettes)**
Messages that are excellent for soul-winning purposes. Proven in the heat of anointing evangelistic efforts.

R101   **GUILTY AS CHARGED**   **3.00** ....
.... A moving drama as Trombley has his day in court complete - with judge, jury, prosecutor and witnesses. Very effective on "700 Club", as a school play and now a book.

R102   **REDEEMING THE WHOLE MAN**   **3.00** ....
.... Justification, sanctification and glorification as seen through the eyes of 1 Cor, 1:10. A balanced, biblical teaching symphonizing Arminism and Calvinism. Excellent insight into the spirit, soul and body of man.

R103   **RIVERS OF BLOOD Side 1**   **3.00** ....
.... **APPLYING THE BLOOD Side 2**
Understanding the value of the blood in removing sin. Follow the trail of blood from Abel to Christ — and beyond revealing it's power over sin, Satan and sickness.... What about pleading the blood? How to resist Satan's attacks.

QUAN.	TITLE	PRICE

12SW **SPIRITUAL WARFARE SERIES**   10.00 ....
.... **(4 cassettes)**
Fight the good fight of faith but how when Satan is so persistent and tricky? This series will take you step by step through His activities unto victory.

S100 **SPOILING THE SPOILER**   3.00 ....
.... Follow Christ as He totally defeats Satan and his kingdom. Until you understand and walk in this truth you'll never have a workable faith. Watch Satan dethroned, his usurped authority restored back to man - for you!

S101 **FLESH VS. DEMONS**   3.00 ....
.... A balanced teaching seperating the flesh from demon activity based on Gal. 5:19-24. Believer's can ignorantly permit Satan to establish a second claim if you don't understand this principle.

S102 **STEPS INTO DEMONISM**   3.00 ....
.... How does satan gain entrance and control? Where do our thoughts come from? What happens when a believer doesn't "steadfastly resist the devil?" Gives the Bible answer for protection.

S103 **DON'T GIVE SATAN**   3.00 ....
.... **THE ADVANTAGE**
Although he has been conquered he retains the power of persuasion. Knowning his "dirty tricks" and God's purposes in allowing them we can step up into God rather than down into defeat.

INDIVIDUAL TAPES

L105 **KEY TO SUBMISSION**   3.00 ....
.... For the ladies. Some practical suggestions on True Grit or True Love. It's working! How to please your husband by one who is one.

L106 **STOP FLAPPING AND START**   3.00 ....
.... **FLYING**
Using Deut. 32:11-14 the eagle is typed showing God's methods of lifting us into the heavenlies. Humorous yet practical. A popular sermon.

R101 **GUILTY AS CHARGED**   3.00 ....
.... A moving drama as Trombley has his day in court. The trial is complete with judge, jury, prosecutor etc. Now a TV play and booklet. Excellent message for the unsaved that works.

IN100 **DON'T FORGET THE BONES**   3.00 ....
.... **—JOSEPH (NEW)**
Seeing the end-time church revealed through the prophetic "bones" of Joseph. The purposes of God for His Body will yet be fulfilled.

P103 **PRAISE IN THE LIFE OF**   3.00 ....
.... **THE BELIEVER**
Study in the Christian priesthood; the sacrifice they offer, and the necessity of attitude of gratitude.

P104 **RESTORATION OF PRAISE**   3.00 ....
.... Study into the restoration of David's Tabernacle (Acts 15:15,16); the restoring of God's dwelling place and the resulting revival already in progress. Prophetic and exciting.

CHARLES TROMBLEY MINISTRIES
293 W. Ithica,   Broken Arrow, OK 74012   251-7290

NAME _____

ADDRESS _____

CITY_____

STATE_____ZIP_____

Tape $_____
Books $_____
Total $_____

Okla. res. add 4%
sales tax $_____

Postage- Books .27 $_____
Tapes .15 $_____

**PLEASE ADD MY NAME TO MAILING
LIST FOR SWORD OF THE SPIRIT.**